THE WAY OF HAPPINESS:
A READING OF WORDSWORTH

By the same author

THOMAS HARDY
THE QUINTESSENCE OF BERNARD SHAW
BEAUTY, TRUTH AND HUMOUR.

THE SOLITARY, THE WANDERER AND THE POET
from the oil-painting by Delmar Banner

THE WAY OF HAPPINESS

A READING OF WORDSWORTH

BY

HENRY CHARLES DUFFIN

SIDGWICK AND JACKSON LIMITED

First published in 1947

PRINTED IN GREAT BRITAIN
BY WESTERN PRINTING SERVICES LTD., BRISTOL

CONTENTS

Two Acknowledgements		vii
Chapter I	A Preliminary Survey of the Way	1
Chapter II	Wordsworth's Experience of the Way	11
Chapter III	Poetry along the Way	49
Chapter IV	Some Studies of the Way:	
	i Love	60
	ii Peace	67
	iii God	71
	iv Physical Happiness	86
	v Beauty	92
	vi Truth	103
Chapter V	The Necessity of Happiness	112
Indexes		124

To Dorothy
*my sweet companion
along the way*

TWO ACKNOWLEDGEMENTS

I AM indebted to my friend H.B.L., who read the manuscript, and by his mulish reluctance to see what I was driving at compelled me to elucidate myself at several points, with a view to making it plain from the outset that this is not a book about Wordsworth, but a book about a single aspect of Wordsworth, about the guidance or illumination afforded by Wordsworth along the road of happiness. Most poets, like most moralists, have allowed themselves to acquiesce in the judgment of Shakespeare's drunken and cynical porter that the primrose way leads to the everlasting bonfire. Wordsworth thought better of primroses, and is in consequence an outstanding exception to the rule that sweetest song tells of saddest thought. His divinest utterance flies on the wings of joy, and he is wisest when he speaks of happy things.

L.'s comments reminded me too of another exceptional fact about Wordsworth, that he excites a personal hostility in the minds of some genuine lovers of literature. At one point in the script L. exclaimed marginally, "Thank goodness for a laugh at the solemn poet!" The remark seems to issue from a sense of irritation which is perhaps a little unreasonable. It is a habit of major poets to take themselves seriously: only Chaucer, Shakespeare, Byron break the rank. And great poetry has always been essentially serious: it is only in comparatively recent times that Mr. de la Mare and a few other poets have discovered a beauty-humour synthesis which is to all intents a new species. The resentful attitude is apparent again in L.'s comment on Wordsworth at Cambridge—"Sounds a bit of a prig." Doubtless; but it is the price we must pay for Wordsworth: no prig, no *Prelude*!

(I ought to add that L.'s help was by no means all of this refractory nature.)

TWO ACKNOWLEDGEMENTS

The debt which I, in common with other lovers of Wordsworth, owe to that greatest of all Wordsworthians, the late Dr. Ernest de Selincourt, goes beyond computing. If there should ever be brought to light a full-length portrait, by, say, (a somewhat precocious) Frans Hals, of Shakespeare at the age of thirty, it might do for us something like what de Selincourt did when he gave us the original *Prelude*—the poem which sprang, pulsing and raw, pure crude miracle, from the violently creative years—to set side by side with the majestic and slowly evolved work of art which had so long delighted us. The publication of the 1805 *Prelude* stands supreme among all de Selincourt's services to Wordsworth scholarship and criticism, dwarfing even the *Letters* and the *Life of Dorothy*, even the complete text of the *Journals*. In those thirteen books, with all their imperfections, we have Wordsworth unobscured, at the height of his genius; the Wordsworth that Coleridge knew and loved and drew inspiration from; the Wordsworth whose vision of truth and quality of experience, whose gust for life and sense of God, form the primary basis of the present study.

Ambleside, 1943—Hove, 1945

My grateful thanks are due to the Clarendon Press for permission to quote widely from the 1805 Prelude *and the* Letters *of William and Dorothy Wordsworth, and I am deeply indebted to Mr. Delmar Banner for his kind and spontaneous offer to let me use his finely imaginative picture as a frontispiece.*

CHAPTER I

A Preliminary Survey of the Way

"I AM MYSELF . . ." said Wordsworth, speaking at an age when a man is either a fool or a philosopher (and Wordsworth was never, in any sense, a fool)—"I am myself one of the happiest of men"; and from 1798 to about the time when he made this claim to Crabb Robinson in 1812 his poetry is the poetry of happiness. It is not all happy, for which we may be thankful: the proportion is not greater than that of sun to cloud in Lakeland weather. It is not often happy poetry at all; but it is always the poetry of a happy man. It does not contain a philosophy of happiness, or an ethic based on happiness, though it contains materials for both. In so far as Wordsworth had a formulated philosophy it was of the universality of Being—of "something far more deeply interfused"; his ethic was the acceptance and following of impulses caught from nature by sense impressions. What I find in Wordsworth's poetry is happiness itself: it is the poetry of a man who had happiness in his soul, so that, whatever his immediate purpose, happiness keeps breaking through from beneath. Whether he is writing a joyous song like *To the Cuckoo* or a melancholy tale like the Wanderer's tale of Margaret, the imprint of the connoisseur in happiness is never wanting. The *Cuckoo* needs no demonstration—it is happiness dissolved in sunlight and song; of Margaret, the Wanderer says,

> by an especial care
> Her temper had been framed, as if to make
> A Being who by adding love to peace
> Might live on earth a life of happiness.[1]

[1] Sources of quotations will be found at the end of the book; as they are listed in the order of the pages on which they appear, references should be nearly as quick as if they were given in footnotes—to a multiplicity of which I have an objection.

Only a man who knew happiness from the inside would have indicated with such quiet assurance those two indispensable factors, love and peace. (And for proof not only of the truth of the analysis but of the exquisite harmony between the minds of Wordsworth and his sister, there is a letter written after the death of John Wordsworth in which Dorothy says, "He seemed to have been made for the best sort of happiness that is to be found in this world, for his whole delight was in peace and love and the beautiful works of this fair Creation".) From the point of view of theme and treatment, Wordsworth's narrative poems are almost universally sombre, but (apart from *Guilt and Sorrow* and *The Borderers*, which belong to a pre-Wordsworthian Wordsworth) I feel that all are taken up into that larger sense of life which lies behind the great body of lyric and reflective poetry belonging to the supreme period: poetry which breathes a serenity bright as that of a June sky, an impassioned joy wide and deep as the world, and which reaches its peaks of achievement when happiness is its theme or its inspiration. *The Excursion*, with which the period closes, is permeated with "admiration, hope and love"; its spirit is faith in God, Nature and Man; its unity is firmly built into the tranquil happiness of the Wanderer.

The systematic study of happiness has been reserved for recent times—till the advent of writers like Dr. Lin Yu Tang and Mr. J. C. Powys, Bertrand Russell and Hermann Keyserling. Wordsworth's understanding of happiness was direct and intuitive, and his exposition proceeded by means of illuminating poetic flashes. These flashes of light upon happiness are of the very essence of his poetry, so that, as he himself declared, that poetry can be understood only by a happy man. (Here again we may recall, not without relevance, Dorothy's conviction that William's poetry must be *liked* by all *good* people.) His realisation of his happiness not only gave him deeper knowledge but made him willing to speak of it, to share his knowledge and his happiness with others. The popular fallacy is that we are happiest when we are unconscious of our happiness, and a Ducal cynic suggested that men are never either so happy or so unhappy as they think they are; but Coleridge knew better, and declared that it is man's privilege as a reasonable being to know and judge his own happiness; the knowledge and consideration of happiness was, he said, its fruition. And Coleridge saw the part played by happiness in Wordsworth's poetic equipment:

> William . . . joy lifts thy spirit, joy attunes thy voice.

"Joy" is Coleridge's word for happiness: Keyserling says happiness is the adult form of joy, and Coleridge was the eternal child, as Wordsworth was adult from his schooldays. Coleridge defined joy as "a consciousness of entire and therefore well-being, when the emotional and intellectual faculties are in equipoise". This implies a harmony of being that comes very near to happiness. To Wordsworth joy was the nucleus of happiness, what he calls elsewhere "blind love", an almost abstract principle, entering into the life of man, of nature, and of cosmic reality.

Happiness, to Wordsworth, was certainly something more than joy. Regard that great poem, *The Happy Warrior*. It might have been called *The Happy Man*. The only lines which definitely relate it to war are those mentioning pain, fear and bloodshed; and even these can be given an application to the contingencies of normal life by reading—

> Who, even when brought in company with Pain,
> And Fear and Bloodshed,

instead of "Who, doomed to go . . ." If then the happy warrior is the happy man, you have no bad definition of happiness in the expression,

> an inward light
> Which makes the path before him ever bright,

and something of a description of the total effect of the happy man in the lines,

> Whose powers shed round him in the common strife
> And mild concerns of ordinary life
> A constant influence, a peculiar grace;
> But who, if he be called upon to face

> Some awful moment to which Heaven has joined
> Great issues, good or bad for human kind,
> Is happy as a lover, and attired
> With sudden brightness, like a man inspired.

That is the nearest analogy that the state of happiness, as Wordsworth conceived it, will bear: an inward light, shining at all times from its possessor and shedding a peculiar grace; sometimes flaming up to a brilliance of inner illumination, but never going out. The terms "*ever* bright" and "a *constant* influence" are to be noted, for happiness, like religion, like life itself, is continuous or nothing.

Continuity in happiness, by resolving emotional discords and making possible a spiritual harmony and a psychological balance, produces serenity, and serenity is doubtless the characteristic of happiness in Wordsworth. Intensity, which is to serenity as soul to body, is there too, but in its Wordsworthian form. Wordsworth's nightingale is almost alone among the nightingales of poetry in neither expressing nor prompting sorrow by its song, but he contrasts the "fierce harmony" that bursts from the "fiery heart" of the nightingale with the "pensive wooing" of the stock-dove:

> He sang of love, with quiet blending,
> Slow to begin, and never ending,
> Of serious faith, and inward glee;

and he expresses his own adherence to the mood of the homelier bird. But there is no less intensity in a quiet and never-ending love than in one that is swift and tumultuous; and the expressions "serious faith" and "inward glee", quaint though they are, do carry just that silent-running depth of still passion which is the reality of both love and happiness. To Wordsworth, as to Fra Lippo, though less light-heartedly, life was no blot nor blank, but meant intensely and meant good. He did not merely delight in the rainbow: his heart leapt up when he saw it in the sky. Verse drove him "like a tempest strong", and left him "a withered flower". He knew "strange fits of passion", and if he went nutting must do so with "merciless ravage". His mortal nature trembled before high instincts, and his thoughts at sight of a common flower were sometimes too deep for tears. Out of this intensity of feeling arose the enormous importance of memory in his life: the undying visions of the daffodils and of the banks of sylvan Wye, of sunrise over Hawkshead and cloudscape on Snowdon, of wayside encounters, London sights, and a hundred pictures recorded in brilliant detail by the camera of his brain. There are, he says,

> There are in our existence spots of time
> Which with distinct pre-eminence retain
> A vivifying virtue.

This life-giving property of the remembered past inheres in the intensity with which the "time-spots" were experienced in the first place.

Intensity of living implies some degree of simplicity, both of life and of mind. During the great productive years Wordsworth's income was low enough to compel simplicity of life, and to make it easy for him to indulge the Athenian virtue characterised by Thucydides as "a love of beauty on small means". But Dorothy's *Journals* show how little compulsion was necessary—with what rapturous intensity brother and sister took hold of the bare elements of the poetic life: loving companionship, the writing and reading of verse, walking in beautiful country. J. S. Mill noted the "perfect simplicity of Wordsworth's character"; and of him at sixty-nine Mrs. Thomas Arnold wrote in praise of "the true humility and simplicity of his mind". Humility has a divine grace of its own, and only a misunderstanding of his attitude to criticism makes it difficult to see humility in Wordsworth, but humility is perhaps not necessary to happiness. Simplicity of mind, of which humility is a derivative, is essential to direct contact with life. A modern tendency of thought is to suppose simplicity—of life, of personality, of religion, of art—to be a primitive condition. Garrod, dealing with this dominating feature in Wordsworth's mind, points out that simplicity is, on the contrary, a flower of civilisation. It implies design, order, control. It is to your "complexity" as monogamy is to sexual promiscuity. Nothing is truer of Wordsworth's poetry than what he himself claimed, that it constitutes a single fabric, designed under one architectonic principle. Only in Milton and Shelley do we find a like singleness of vision with similar unifying effect. And if this simplicity and singleness implies a certain narrowness, it is a narrowness that cuts deep, giving that vital touch upon reality which is perhaps the profoundest source of happiness.

There is a certain unselfconscious directness of relation which is to-day much out of fashion, though still having its attraction, to judge by a pleasant fragment of verse by Mr. A. L. Rowse:

> Perhaps life is simpler than I thought
> (I thought), simple and promising as a smile
> From the driver of an ambulance or tank
> To the admiring girl in the street.

This kind of simplicity has always had deep significance for the poets, but its nearest equivalent in Wordsworth is a happiness seemingly simple and yet analysable into peace, love and thought: on his return to Hawkshead for his first Cambridge vacation he says,

> When first I made
> Once more the circuit of our little lake,
> If ever happiness hath lodged with man
> That day consummate happiness was mine,
> Wide-spreading, steady, calm, contemplative.

Happiness, to Wordsworth, is to be "a simple produce of the common day"; it arises in no small degree from "little, nameless, unremembered acts of kindness and of love". It is inseparable from the way of nature—

> The wisest, happiest of our kind are they
> Who ever walk content with Nature's way.

It hardly needs to be said that "nature", as a way of life, must be purged and purified by being passed through the civilised mind before it can become the sure accompaniment of happiness and wisdom. What Wordsworth means by "Nature's way" may be known by reference to some other lines where he speaks of Dorothy as being "attuned to Nature"

> By her benign simplicity of life,
> And through a perfect happiness of soul.

He knows how simplicity and singleness are twisted and broken by the lure of that glittering thing, success, and writes of men who,

> Having known the splendours of success,
> Sigh for the obscurities of happiness.

I am reminded of a glowing fragment of anonymous prose in which William and Dorothy, at Racedown, at Alfoxden, at Dove Cottage, would have delighted: "If the night and the day are such that you greet them with joy, and life emits a fragrance like flowers or sweet scented herbs, is more elastic, more starry, more immortal—that is your success".

Of all the constituents of happiness we have so far considered—love and peace, serenity and simplicity, even joy—only love has a positive and active content. And though love in all its normal manifestations was, as we shall see later, almost co-terminous with Wordsworth's happiness, only one aspect calls for notice at this stage—that "blind love" already named as the hidden root of happiness. The unique and unmistakable condition of the soul which we call happiness is, in its entirety, too complex to submit to definition, yet if we are seeking the very nature of its life, the essential truth of its quality, we shall find something thoroughly satisfying in the two lines by which Wordsworth indicates the response made by his shepherd Michael to the fields and hills amidst which he worked:

> A pleasurable feeling of blind love,
> The pleasure which there is in life itself.

Love particularised, whether human or divine, may bring almost infinite pain: "blind love", a passionate going out of the whole being in ecstasy to "life itself", is the indestructible core of happiness. It is characteristic of Wordsworth's genius that this definitive expression of his uttermost feeling is attached to an inarticulate rustic, and therefore clothed in the simplest terms, terms so unemphatic that the importance of the statement has been generally overlooked. The mild epithet "pleasurable" in the first line is nicely adapted to the undeveloped mind of the peasant: in other contexts "ecstatic" would have been more appropriate, and "intense" or "profound" would be required before "pleasure" in the second line. The "pleasure", for Wordsworth and those who can share his feeling, is a complex emotion, comprising animal sensation, an intellectual appreciation of that sensation, thankfulness for the miracle of life, and a vague but passionate worship. But if the elements of that subtle diagnosis, in its plain original form, are grasped in their entirety and essence, they will be found to give the central truth of Wordsworth's conception of happiness, round which all the other features build themselves.

The miraculous pleasure of this blind love is rooted in the joy of earth, and is inevitably accompanied by a belief in nature dimly sentient and for the most part happy—the faith of the *Lines Written in Early Spring*, that not only the birds but the primroses and the budding twigs take pleasure in the young sunshine. For the birds, scientific observers are prone to insist on the sufferings of the animal creation (just as to the moralist the life of man is a vale of tears), and Wordsworth would not have denied that there are flaws in "Nature's holy plan". But he would have advised us to do our own observing. "Watch the brown trout hanging in the current of the Rothay," he would have said, with the approval of any naturalist without an axe to grind; "watch the insects in the grass, the birds in the trees, the rabbits on the commons, and you will know that for every moment of fear or agony there are hours of busy enjoyment." Even the extension of his belief to the flowers and the green life of nature must persuade anyone but a hardened materialist. Doubtless the pleasure felt by any individual leaf is smaller than that experienced by a millionaire when he finds a penny, but when you consider the number of leaves and flowers, bracken fronds and blades of grass within Wordsworth's sight as he sat in his grove that Spring morning, it may be that the aggregate of joy was commensurable with what the poet felt in observing it, though doubtless different in kind.

What of the suggestion made by Mr. Aldous Huxley, and taken up by John Buchan, Mr. Ivor Brown and others, that if Wordsworth had known the tropical jungle his philosophy of nature would have been different? The possibility has to be considered, but consideration leaves the realism of Wordsworth's outlook undamaged. It was in the Lake District that he learnt to love and admire mankind, too: afterwards, in France, he waded breast-high through monstrous jungle-growths of human nature, but his faith in man survived the experience, as it had survived the lesser disillusionments of Cambridge and London. We need not suppose that his faith in nature was less virile and resistant. Why, again, limit Wordsworth's nature-lore to that acquired in the English lakes?—at least he had crossed the Alps on foot, and known terror in the wild and gloomy Gondo. Why, finally, foist upon him a belief that even among the Fells nature is always kindly? He had seen exquisite children like Lucy Gray, and the parents of innocent children like the Greenes, savagely slain by his own northern winters and wilds. His creed did not necessitate a nature uniformly benign. His claims were—that all nature, animate and inanimate, shared in that "principle of joy" which man himself overmuch neglected; that the spirit of nature, imaginatively known, could be an inspiring companion to the human spirit; that nature was a manifestation of the Being of God. I do not see that any of these claims is invalidated by change in latitude. If Wordsworth saw pleasure in the budding of a twig he would have seen a Bacchanalian revel in the lush luxuriance of tropical vegetation. W. H. Hudson, who did know the jungle, insisted that animal life, though from time to time "red in tooth and claw", was full of busy enjoyment terminated only by the short unselfconscious pang of death. Wordsworth might have drawn inspiration from giant forests as Lawrence did from the Valley of Rumm, and have felt the pulse of Being throbbing feverishly or magnificently in the jungle. It does not appear, from the Vedas and Upanishads, that poets of tropical regions were driven to evolve a cruel conception of the gods from their observation of nature, while Tagore's poetic vision of "creative unity" is closely related to Wordsworth's. Objection comes from those who have worked or fought under tropical conditions, but their approach is fallacious. You must live according to nature, under whatever skies. If you defy her strength she will strike you down; if you pursue the unnatural business of industrialised commerce or "civilised" war in the desert or the jungle, you cannot expect nature to be consenting to your folly.

In a sense Nature was Wordsworth's religion. His days were bound each to each by natural piety. His heart leaped when he saw a rainbow as the heart of the Christian is stirred by the story of the Cross. But he could not stop at nature. That would have left him a materialist, and a materialist can only be superficially happy. Arising out of the religion of nature preached so persuasively by Rousseau, an outlook bearing some resemblance to pantheism is widespread in the literature and thought of the end of the eighteenth century, but Wordsworth's instinct of mystery at the unfathomable heart of things ensured that with him pantheism should rest on an underlying but never forgotten sense of a God supreme, aloof, and unknowable. Nevertheless his "efficient" faith, both poetic and religious, was in the mystically known reality of God which is the substance and significance of all phenomena, "natural" and other. The knowledge of this reality, and the sense of mystic contact with it, can give a purer happiness than that which can arise from any non-mystic religion; and Wordsworth possessed this knowledge and this sense in a form peculiarly conducive to happiness, for he perceived in the numinous reality of life a positive tendency, a purposive spirit, which he recognised as "joy". Hence the last, and in some ways the most vital, factor in happiness was, for Wordsworth, doubly right.

CHAPTER II

Wordsworth's Experience of the Way

HAPPINESS DOES NOT come out of experience, but experience out of happiness. Happiness, a spiritual state, must proceed from a spiritual origin. Wordsworth's happiness was primarily of temperament, and temperament, though affected by physical factors, is in itself spiritual, being as it were the colour of the mind. Coleridge thought Wordsworth's happiness was philosophical, but philosophy would (perhaps) have carried Wordsworth through the afflictions of 1812, the loss of the two beloved children. It was temperament that Wordsworth had in view when he made the celebrated avowal to Crabb Robinson, and again when, twenty years later, he spoke of certain "genial feelings" which had been "a vital principle of my existence". He himself recognised two temperamental aspects:

> Having two natures in me, joy the one,
> The other melancholy, and withal
> A happy man.

His conclusion shows that the "joyous nature" preponderated; and in early life, at all events, he was, like Jaques, capable of watching the operations of his melancholy with some enjoyment.

It is not simply that temperament colours experience as a landscape is different under the light of sun and moon; temperament profoundly modifies the will to life, and the will to life affects the whole shape and texture of life. It was the will to life that kept Wordsworth from being a hack parson, and enabled him and Dorothy to find riches in £130 a year. In the main his happiness was the "inward light", but that light is only half used if it does not make bright the path through life, and there was in fact a great deal more happiness in Wordsworth's life than is sometimes admitted. I propose to view the picture through the lens of happiness, which will bring out the warmer colours and suppress the cold shades. This will cause some shifting of values, but not, I think, distortion, and I want to put it beyond doubt that Wordsworth's understanding of happiness was based upon an amplitude of happy experience as well as on the intuition of genius, which can work on the slenderest basis of observation. Art criticism gains if the critic has produced at least a few good pictures: the poetry of happiness will come best from a poet whose life has been substantially happy. In Wordsworth's case poetry itself came out of, or ran parallel with, experience of happiness.

Yet temperament itself is formed, or partly formed, by one part of experience, by the semiconscious but wholly receptive experience of childhood and early youth. It may be that the darker side of Wordsworth's nature was congenital, but his happy temperament was established by a childhood which included not only the normal fostering elements of kindly treatment and freedom from want, but the less usual circumstances of beauty of environment and a quite extraordinary degree of liberty. No poetry exceeds in nostalgic fervour the passages in which Wordsworth refers to the natural scenery of his childhood's home:

> Was it for this
> That one, the fairest of all rivers, loved
> To blend his murmurs with my nurse's song,
> And from his alder shades and rocky falls
> And from his fords and shallows sent a voice
> That flowed along my dreams? For this didst thou,
> O Derwent! travelling over the green plains
> Near my "sweet Birthplace", didst thou, beauteous Stream,
> Make ceaseless music that composed my thoughts
> To more than infant softness.

But the grand formative of happy temperament is freedom during the period of youth. The happiness which filled the first half of Wordsworth's life and inspired so much of his best poetry was primarily due, I believe, to the freedom he enjoyed during his nine years as a Hawkshead schoolboy. Physical freedom he owed to wise, kindly, complaisant Dame Tyson, and mental freedom to the easy-going system of education in vogue at Hawkshead. Mr. Logan Pearsall Smith, in that subtle piece of autobiography, *Unforgotten Years*, depicts a childhood almost equally free, and calls that childhood a happy prelude to a happy life.

Wordsworth's liberties were already wide in very early years:

> Oh, many a time have I, a five years' child,
> A naked boy, in one delightful rill,
> A little mill-race severed from his stream,
> Made one long bathing of a summer's day
>   ... or coursed
> Over the sandy fields ... or stood alone
> Beneath the sky, as if I had been born
> On Indian plains.

But it was the freedom enjoyed during the adolescent years that both gave him his first realised experience of happiness and conditioned his temperament for many years to come. It is notorious that although Wordsworth devoted one whole Book of the *Prelude* and portions of several others to his schooldays he never once refers to the instruction he must have received within the narrow walls of Hawkshead Grammar School. The *Prelude* tells us that he possessed an abridged copy of the *Arabian Nights*, that in the holidays he found at home "a golden store of books" open to his enjoyment, and that he and another boy used to walk by Esthwaite's misty borders "repeating favourite verses". We know that his father made him learn much poetry by heart. But regular tuition he dismisses with the words,

>   easily indeed
> We might have fed upon a fatter soil
> Of arts and letters, but be that forgiven:

And forgiven it certainly was, for he speaks with pity and

contempt of boys who, subject to a severer system, became prodigies of learning. And many years later, in rebuking an Inspector of Schools for worrying about the wear and tear of children's clothes, he said he spoke as one who spent half his boyhood running wild upon the mountains.

Run wild he did. Before morning school (though this began at six o'clock in summer) he would walk round Esthwaite Lake; and even earlier, "at the first hour of dawn-light", would be sitting alone on some eminence jutting over the vale. At the other end of the day he was accustomed "to wander half the night among the cliffs" setting springes for woodcocks. In between these two extremes came bird-nesting on the lonesome peaks, long excursions into distant vales, skating at six on winter evenings, and games prolonged till sunset in summer. Well could he say,

> We ran a boisterous race. The year span round
> With giddy motion;

and again,

> I might pursue this theme through every change
> Of exercise and play, to which the year
> Did summon us in its delightful round.

He insists on the happiness that attended this spacious life:

> We were a noisy crew; the sun in heaven
> Beheld not vales more beautiful than ours;
> Nor saw a band in happiness and joy
> Richer, or worthier of the ground they trod;

describing himself and his schoolfellows elsewhere as "in happiness not yielding to the happiest on earth". My submission is that these years of free enjoyment so strengthened and developed the joyous element in his moral constitution that he was able to traverse the valley of political and philosophical despair and emerge into a period of almost unique happiness to produce a poetry of happiness that is altogether unique.

The temporary descent into the shadow was not to come for

some years yet. To the freedom of Hawkshead succeeded the freedom of Cambridge, and the picture Wordsworth gives of his University life in the *Prelude* is painted almost entirely in bright colours. He went up in high and hopeful spirits, and entered upon the busy doings of the freshman "with loose and careless heart".

> I was the Dreamer, they the Dream; I roamed
> Delighted through the motley spectacle.

With no less delight he looked upon "those many happy youths", for, says he, "my heart was social and loved idleness and joy". So that in spite of "now and then forced labour" he was moved to exclaim, "This was a gladsome time", and able to record that he returned for his second year "gay and undepressed in spirit". When Dorothy visited Cambridge a few months later she found William "very well and in excellent spirits". Looking back on his University days from a distance of forty years he said he had been "as joyous as a lark". (But then—don't we all?)

It was not only a matter of "invitations, suppers, wine and fruit", and a continuation of the boisterous schooltime activities. He knew a joy far deeper than any the ordinary undergraduate could know. He was a chosen son, and felt within himself holy powers and faculties.[1]

> I was a Freeman; in the purest sense
> Was free, and to majestic ends was strong.

Though unknown and undistinguished he felt rich—

> I had a world about me; 'twas my own,
> I made it.

He made it out of "a childlike fruitfulness in passing joy", out of steady moods of thoughtfulness matured to inspiration. Yes,

> The Poet's soul was with me at that time,
> Sweet meditations, the still overflow
> Of happiness and truth.

[1] It is here that H.B.L. sees "priggishness".

A thousand hopes and tender dreams were his, and as he remembers them at the age of four-and-thirty, he is able to say,

> And yet the morning gladness is not gone
> Which then was on my mind.

Of a darker side to the picture Wordsworth gives but the smallest hints. He was disturbed by occasional thoughts of what the "relatives" expected of him, so that the independent course he was following looked like "an act of disobedience". And he notes a melancholy in himself that loved to dwell on the sadder aspects of nature, but which was in fact a subtle source of pleasure, being "a treasured and luxurious gloom", and the "mere redundancy of youth's contentedness".

Superimposed upon the faintly adulterated joys of Cambridge terms were the pure happiness, and the pure freedom, of the vacations.

> In summer among distant nooks I roved,
> Dovedale, or Yorkshire Dales, or through bye-tracts
> Of my own native regions, and was blest
> Between these sundry wanderings with a joy
> Above all joys, that seemed another morn
> Risen on mid-noon.

This was the joy of spending weeks with Dorothy at Penrith, roaming the countryside, climbing about the ruins of Brougham Castle, reading together the parts already written of *An Evening Walk*, William's first ambitious poem, to be dedicated to Dorothy. At other times he walked with Mary there, and he felt that over all the woodlands and lanes, the crags and the fells, there were scattered love and the spirit of pleasure and youth's golden gleam. Presently came the great walk through France and the Alps with his fellow student, Jones. Towards its conclusion he wrote to his sister, "I am in excellent health and spirits, and have had no reason to complain of the contrary during our whole tour. My spirits have been kept in a perpetual hurry of delight." Moreover, in William's imagination, already that marvellous sharing of every thought and emotion had begun: "I have thought of you perpetually", he writes; "and never have my eyes burst upon a scene of particular loveliness but I have almost instantly wished that you could for a moment be transplanted to the place where I stood to enjoy it." The historical moment was auspicious to the happiness of a young republican mind like Wordsworth's, for France stood "on the top of golden hours", and the joy of one was the joy of tens of millions. (Wordsworth seems to show, by his use of this phrasing, that he was not of a mind with those unimaginative people who declare that a million happy people are no happier than one happy person.) As the two young men walked they found "benevolence and blessedness spread like a fragrance everywhere", and when rejoicing France was left behind they began to cross "sweet coverts of pastoral life", where the heart of at least one of them leaped to see the "sanctified abodes of peaceful Man". Here was a book of simple feeling, of real life, in which were to be read leassons of tenderness, reason and truth. If moments of depression came, they were "taken up for pleasure's sake" and served to "sweeten many a meditative hour". And all this, remember—for Wordsworth, with whom walking was a passion—to the tune of "thirteen leagues a day". The only suggestion of a "sterner mood" occurs in that brief dejection which fell upon the travellers when they found they had crossed the ridge of the Alps unawares: a strange seizure of the imagination which ended in an access of joy. Indeed, in his lofty poet's way, Wordsworth felt that the total effect of his experiences in "that magnificent region" had been to help him forward and "administer to grandeur and to tenderness". But he did not need this æsthetic satisfaction any more than he needed the political hopes which were then abroad: he was happy in himself:

> I needed not that joy, I did not need
> Such help; the everliving Universe
> And independent spirit of pure youth
> Were with me at that season, and delight
> Was in all places spread around my steps
> As constant as the grass upon the fields.

Some weeks of intense happiness with Dorothy at Forncett Rectory preceded the new adventure of a plunge into London life. He remained in London only four or five months, and from letters written immediately afterwards, and the later backward-glances of the *Prelude*, appears to have been sufficiently happy alone in the great city, "Free as a colt at pasture in the hills". He went to London, "if not in calmness" (for he was still undecided as to a career), at least undisturbed by personal ambition or excessive hope. He calls the "motley imagery" which passed before his eyes (in a passage afterwards excised—though not till about 1840)

> A vivid pleasure of my youth, and now,
> Among the lonely places that I love,
> A frequent day-dream for my riper mind.

He found delight in the theatre, and savoured the peace and solemnity of night in London, the calm beauty of moonlight on empty streets. His only record of pain and distress occurs in connection with the women he saw degraded to blasphemy and vice by city life.

These "recollected emotions" of the *Prelude* serve to show Wordsworth sustained by inward happiness in uncongenial surroundings, and for more immediate testimony we have a letter written to Mathews from Wales, in which he says, "I quitted London about three weeks ago, where my time passed in a strange manner; sometimes whirled about by the vortex of its *strenua inertia*, and sometimes thrown by the eddy into a corner of the stream, where I lay in motionless indolence. Think not however that I had not many very pleasant hours." Moreover, there was constantly with him the under-sense of power, turning the flowing crowds into a dream-procession of mysterious significance. The inspiration of nature lived unchanged in his heart, giving him "high thoughts of God and man", a certain "complacency", love for his fellow beings, and "motions of delight". Speaking to Coleridge he says, "I did not pine as thou didst—one in city bred"; for he had "forms distinct" to steady him, "a real solid world of images about me", the tranquillising images of Cumbrian hills and lakes.

During the months which followed, with Jones in Wales, he was sure enough of himself to give advice on happiness. Writing again to Mathews in August he said he was sorry to hear that his friend's share of happiness was so small; he attributed to fatigue "that depression of spirits which disposes you to look on the dark side of things", and suggested that if he could release himself from irksome toil his spirits would become cheerful and he would see things in a more favourable light. Mathews evidently wrote for further encouragement, and Wordsworth advised him not to let dissatisfaction take root. Avoid, he said, dead-ends in life. "Let hope be your walking-staff, and your fortune is made."

Wordsworth was now on the verge of that period, covering the years 1792, 1793, and most of 1794, into which was concentrated almost all the experience of unhappiness that he knew in his early manhood. His principal biographer and some of his critics think that it was largely because of what he underwent in this period, and of the subsequent emotional stress, that he became one of the voices of the age. Wordsworth himself attached less importance to these years. "I passed the time", he said of them in the biographical notes dictated to Ida Fenwick in later life, "among my friends in London and elsewhere"—nothing more than that. This lack of emphasis bears out my own view of the period and its results: these latter were, I believe, not deeper or more permanent than those of a physical illness from which the patient in time completely recovers. France, and the French Revolution, and all that they meant for Wordsworth, helped to fill and enrich and discipline his mind. But so, and more amply, did Hawkshead, Cambridge, Racedown, Alfoxden, Grasmere.

We begin with the year spent in France, between Paris, Orleans and Blois, from December 1791 to the end of 1792. His experiences in France had two sides, political and erotic, both productive of immediate but short-lived happiness. Wordsworth was already a Republican at heart, and having quickly become a "Patriot", his heart "all given to the people", he must have derived the richest satisfaction from his intimacy with Beaupuy. To some extent he was able to ignore the crude externals of the Revolution, and remained "Tranquil, almost, and careless as a flower Glassed in a green-house". He accepted the September massacres, "lamentable crimes, 'tis true"—though in Paris he passed a sleepless night thinking about the possibility of their repetition—and continued "enflamed with hope". The quality of his feeling about the Revolution at this time, as well as his capacity for intense happiness, are unmistakably shown in the great passage of the *Prelude* beginning,

> O pleasant exercise of hope and joy!
> For great were the auxiliars which then stood
> Upon our side, we who were strong in love;
> Bliss was it in that dawn to be alive,
> But to be young was very heaven!

And side by side with this vivid political life we are to suppose there was going on a tale of young hearts in love. Like scientists studying the behaviour of the atom, we have to make our inferences from observed consequences, for of the thing itself we see nothing. The accounts which have been written of the episode are as insubstantial as the life-story of Shakespeare. We know that a baby was born to William Wordsworth and Annette Vallon in December 1792, and that Annette wrote passionate letters in the next year to William and Dorothy. But of the relations between Annette and the young poet during the year he was in France we know just nothing. We have three of Wordsworth's letters written from France, two to brother Richard and one to Mathews: none of them shows any sign of emotional distraction either political or amatory; all of them display a mind cheerfully engaged with normal activities. The *Prelude* as nearly as possible ignores Annette. Having described his political experiences in the greatest detail, Wordsworth says in effect, "I could go on for a long time about this, but instead I will repeat to you a tale told me by my friend Beaupuy". He proceeds to tell the tale of Vaudracour and Julia, which bears a very remote resemblance to that of William and Annette. Almost the only sign that it was prompted by his own story is to be seen in his anxiety, in the revision of 1820, to emphasise that the illicit union was deliberately and rationally entered upon, not brought about by "the effect of some unguarded moment that dissolved Virtuous restraint". It would seem likely that the marvellous passage—

> Arabian fiction never filled the world
> With half the wonders that were wrought for him.
> Earth breathed in one great presence of the Spring;
> Life turned the meanest of her implements
> Before his eyes to price above all gold;
> The house she dwelt in was a sainted shrine;
> Her chamber window did surpass in glory
> The portals of the dawn; all paradise
> Could, by the simple opening of a door,
> Let itself in upon him; pathways, walks,
> Swarmed with enchantment, till his spirit sank
> Surcharged within him,—overblest to move
> Beneath a sun that wakes a weary world
> To its dull round of ordinary cares;
> A man too happy for mortality!—

it would seem likely that this at least gives a true picture of Wordsworth's feelings in the early months of 1792. It is certainly the only passage in Wordsworth which might find a place in *Romeo and Juliet*. What a supreme line is that—"Earth breathed in one great presence of the Spring"; and how wonderfully, after the traditional raptures over the house and the chamber-window, comes the new vision of a miracle personally experienced: "all paradise Could by the simple opening of a door Let itself in upon him".

And yet this passage does not, I think, belong with Sappho and Shakespeare, with Burns and Browning. Is it love poetry at all? Is the passionate feeling that inspires it love, or even the love of love, at all? Is it not rather love of life—sheer Wordsworthian happiness again? Indeed, a good deal more than

Annette went to the composition of this tale, in its two versions of 1805 and 1820. Going a little farther back in the poem, we have a passage about a youth and a girl growing up together—

> Each other's advocate, each other's stay,
> And strangers to content if long apart—

which strongly suggests William and Dorothy, especially when amplified in 1820 by the simile of the pair of sea-birds "parted and reunited by the blast" which he had used in *The Recluse* to describe the wintry walk over the Sedbergh heights on the way to Grasmere. In the next few lines he seems to say, This was the true basis of an enduring love (that is, the love between William and Dorothy), but for the moment Vaudracour (William) was under a temporary "fascination" by a present object —"the thing he saw". A passage of singular beauty added for the 1820 version has a more authentic sound of young love than anything else in the poem. Speaking of "a stolen interview Accomplished under friendly shade of night", the poet says,

> Through all her courts
> The vacant City slept; the busy winds,
> That keep no certain intervals of rest,
> Moved not; meanwhile the galaxy displayed
> Her fires, that like mysterious pulses beat
> Aloft;—momentous but uneasy bliss!
> To their full hearts the universe seemed hung
> On that brief meeting's slender filament!

That reads like a record of something experienced. But it was not put down when the *Prelude* was being written! It is as if Wordsworth, now nearly fifty, looked back and recaptured a moment which in 1804 he had desired impatiently to "pass".

His omission of Annette from among the influences which assisted in the "growth of the poet's mind" may indicate that he regarded the "incident" of his union with her as belonging to the same order as the occasion when he took too much wine at St. John's. Before he died he seems to have forgotten her altogether: "I wonder why I stayed in France so long?" he asked musingly in 1849. The familiar picture of him fretting to get back to France to "regularise" the union is based not upon any printed evidence (other than Carlyle's inconclusive report), but upon the assumption that he would want to do what any young man of normal moral outlook would have wanted to do. But, as the uncles well knew, William's moral outlook was not normal. Dorothy's letters to Jane Pollard in 1793 are full of concentrated William, but betray no expectation that he is likely to do anything so upsetting as to marry the French woman to whom she was writing words of sympathy and consolation. In short, it does not appear that Annette contributed vitally either to what happiness Wordsworth found in France in 1792 or to the unhappiness of that year and the two succeeding ones. She was, as Garrod suggests, not important. Whether, even so, William would not have done better to marry her is a question to which I shall return. For the moment, his own comment was made in *The Borderers* a year or two afterwards:

> Action is transitory—a step, a blow,
> A motion of a muscle—this way or that—
> 'Tis done; and in the after-vacancy
> We wonder at ourselves like men betrayed.

Whatever the attitude Wordsworth took towards the relationship with Annette, the situation at the end of 1792 cannot have left him other than uneasy, especially when he had to explain (by letter—a letter that has not been preserved) to Dorothy, with the request that she should break the news to her uncle, the Canon of Windsor. On Dorothy the effect seems to have been completely negligible, so far as her estimation of her erring brother was concerned. None of her letters about her "beloved William" are more passionately enthusiastic—"blinded", as she confesses—than those written to her friend Jane in June and July 1793. But Uncle Cookson was not pleased, and for six months William skulked under a cloud of family disapprobation. His uneasiness on the personal count was converted into violent unhappiness by the English declaration of war on the new Republic. So in August he grasped at the grand remedy for all unhappiness, a walking tour. Leaving Calvert on Salisbury Plain he walked into South Wales via Bath, Bristol and the Wye. By the banks of that already immortal river he listened to the waters rolling from their mountain source with a soft inland murmur, while the secluded scene impressed thoughts of more deep seclusion and connected the landscape with the quiet of the sky. But it was something more than quiet thoughts that came to refresh his soul by sylvan Wye. Here was the loveliness of wood, water and mountain that he most loved: he plunged headlong in, and emerged aching with joy, dizzy with rapture. He found what he had almost forgotten, that nature to him was all in all: what haunted him now like a passion was not the state of France, nor Annette, nor anxiety about his position, but the sounding cataract, the tall rock, the mountain and the deep and gloomy wood. For these he had been hungry: with these his appetite was now sated. Such transcendental happiness as this had to wait five years before Wordsworth was poet enough to find language for it.

He joined Dorothy at Halifax. And here, doubtless, infinite as was his delight in her company, his mind was too deeply disturbed to find complete happiness. He had been, not long before this, tempted aside from his instinctive love of man and faith in man to an alien philosophy, with the result that he lost

> All feeling of conviction, and in fine,
> Sick, wearied out with contrarieties,
> Yielded up moral questions in despair.

The Terror in France had broken out afresh in monstrous form, and whether or not Wordsworth looked again upon some of its brutalities with his own eyes, his soul was lacerated by the discovery that what he had believed so beneficent had stooped to means so dreadful. And still the problem of his future and Dorothy's remained unsettled. So once again he summoned walking to his aid, and this time he walked with Dorothy—"our first pilgrimage", she afterwards called it. Taking coach to Kendal they walked through to Keswick, where they had been offered farmhouse accommodation at Windy Brow by

William Calvert. To be walking was William's idea of perfect liberty, and now he had the companionship of Dorothy on one of the loveliest roads in his beloved Lake country. The combination could not fail to bring happiness; that it did so we have living proof. During the afternoon of the first day's walk (Kendal to Grasmere, eighteen miles) they found themselves on a stretch of the road running close by Windermere shore, and here they paused to rest beside a tiny stream that comes down the hillside a few hundred yards north of the Low Wood Inn. Afterwards William wrote a sonnet to that "little unpretending rill", concluding,

> The immortal spirit of one happy day
> Lingers beside that Rill in vision clear.

The rill still flows, but the road is widened and metalled, and the stream must flow beneath. In 1794 the road was a narrow brown track, quiet to the footfall; and the rill would flow, bright and sweet, across it.

And so, next day, thirteen miles to Keswick and Windy Brow. If Racedown and Alfoxden were to be preliminary try-outs for Dove Cottage, the six weeks or so spent at Windy Brow provided an early sketch of the possibilities. They were not alone, but at least they were free from relatives, and Dorothy found the family at the farmhouse "the most honest, cleanly, sensible people I ever saw in their rank of life, and . . . happier than anybody I know". The two, with their unconquerable hope ever in their minds, must have derived no small pleasure from "calculating from our present expenses for how very small a sum we could live". On the other hand they could not expect to live on nothing, and William's letters for the next half-year are almost totally concerned with efforts, fortunately unsuccessful, to enter the ranks of London journalism. In the meantime he was busying himself with correcting and enlarging the *Evening Walk* and the *Descriptive Sketches*, and with the composition of *Guilt and Sorrow*. And then the miracle fell into Dorothy's lap. Raisley Calvert left William £900, and the way was clear to the cottage of their dreams

THE WAY OF HAPPINESS

That is to anticipate by nearly three-quarters of a year. The way did not become quite clear till John Pinney's offer of a furnished house in Dorset came together with the promise of two or three children to take charge of, and brought their prospective income up to subsistence level. In September 1795 William set out from Bristol, where he had been staying with the Pinneys, to walk to Racedown, the house in Dorset; Dorothy was to join him there by coach. The lines he composed on the way, and afterwards used as a "preamble" to the *Prelude*, strike the tonic note for the period which was to ensue. They are far superior to anything we know Wordsworth had written at this date, and they voice, for the first time, the full mood of happiness.

> Oh there is blessing in this gentle breeze
> That blows from the green fields and from the clouds
> And from the sky: it beats against my cheek,
> And seems half-conscious of the joy it gives.

He has been a prisoner, but now is free, free to turn by road or pathway or through open field, or to follow a wandering cloud or a twig upon the river.

> The earth is all before me: with a heart
> Joyous, nor scared at its own liberty,
> I look about.

The burthen of weary days of unnatural life is miraculously shaken off, so that

> Trances of thought and mountings of the mind
> Come fast upon me.

He feels that he can look forward to long months of peace and ease and undisturbed delight, wherein he may dedicate himself to chosen tasks. And he knows what those tasks are to be, for while the breath of heaven blows on his body he feels within "a corresponding mild creative breeze" which presently became "a tempest, a redundant energy", and could only mean one thing—"The holy life of music and of verse".

Fate, through John Pinney, had sent William and Dorothy to a spot within a day's walk of Ottery St. Mary, the birthplace of Coleridge, but the significance of this fact did not become apparent for nearly two years. Neither did the promise of musical verse fulfil itself at once. But all the other elements of happiness were present in that rent-free charmingly furnished house to which Dorothy always looked back lovingly as to her "first home". She organised the house-work to a wonder, and was assisted in it by "one of the nicest girls I ever saw". William gardened and hewed wood, and they lived on vegetables and by log fires. Little Basil Montagu, the only one of the promised children to materialise, was subjected to a kind, firm, intelligent discipline the aim of which was "to make him *happy*", and thus give his elders leave to be happy too. He was transformed from a spoilt weakling into a hardy, contented, attractive boy—a living proof of the truth that it is generally better for children (certainly "only" children) to be brought up other than by their parents. The neighbours were dull or objectionable, but the tenants of Racedown had a succession of delightful visitors: the Pinney youths, Montagu, Cottle (for publishing), Tom Poole, Citizen Thelwall, Hazlitt and Lamb, Mary Hutchinson—and Coleridge (some of these belong to Alfoxden days).

Yet William's mind was not fully at ease. There were letters from Annette, though probably no one now thought of a marriage. His nights were still disturbed by thoughts of the Revolution lapsed into blood and conquest. He had not recovered from the "shock to his moral nature" caused by the English declaration of war on the Republic. And the joyless doctrines of "Godwin on Necessity" had not yet loosed their hold on his mind. But soon life with Dorothy brought him peace and happiness. It was not only that

> the beloved Sister in whose sight
> Those days were passed, now speaking in a voice
> Of sudden admonition—like a brook
> That did but cross a lonely road, and now
> Is seen, heard, felt, and caught at every turn,
> Companion never lost through many a league—
> Maintained for me a saving intercourse
> With my true self—

THE WAY OF HAPPINESS

It was not only that

> She, in the midst of all, preserved me still
> A Poet, made me seek beneath that name
> My office upon earth, and nowhere else:

of even greater power in the restoring of Wordsworth to happiness was the unique love which was the vital relation between this brother and sister.

That "blind love" of life which lies at the core of the Wordsworthian happiness can arise probably in only two ways—out of mystic religious feeling, or (for a man) out of love for a woman. Both of these causes were operative with Wordsworth. If love for a woman is to bring a "blind love" of life, and hence happiness, it must be passionate, continuous, and permanent, as was William's love for Dorothy (like hers for him). The love between Charles and Mary Lamb was profound, tender and completely normal; it is impossible not to be aware of the strong element of passion which entered, on both sides, into the love of William and Dorothy Wordsworth. There is something almost Greek in this picture of passion without sex: that is to say, without sex in its primary function, but of course not without all that extensive and delightful area of sex which surrounds, embellishes and sublimates the central purpose. To the intensity of the mutual feeling William's poems, Dorothy's *Journals* (more particularly in de Selincourt's full text, for Knight's calculated omissions water the thing down considerably), and the *Letters* bear witness. William loved Mary, and Dorothy loved Coleridge; but if William had been presented with the choice of cutting Mary or Dorothy out of his life, and Dorothy with the choice between Coleridge and William, both would unhesitatingly have answered in the same way. An amusing pointer to William's preference is found in a sentence from the letter to Coleridge written on Christmas Eve 1799: "I arrived at Sockburn the day after you quitted it. . . . I was sadly disappointed in not finding Dorothy; Mary was a solitary housekeeper, and overjoyed to see me". And it is with William's love for Dorothy, not hers for him, that I am here concerned, for

WORDSWORTH'S EXPERIENCE OF THE WAY

Wordsworth's happiness is my text, and it is active love, not being loved, that brings (to a man) happiness in the exalted Wordsworthian sense. If all the love poetry inspired by Dorothy were collected, from the *Prelude*, the *Tintern Abbey* lines, Book I of *The Recluse*, and the minor poems, it would be found to exceed in bulk that written by any other English poet (except perhaps Philip Sidney, Robert Browning and Thomas Hardy) to one woman—that is to say, excluding the wandering flames of Burns and Shelley and the dubious objectives of Shakespeare in the Sonnets.

Outside the poetry, Dorothy perceived William's heart-satisfying intensity of feeling in "a sort of violence of affection, if I may so term it (she is writing in 1793 to Jane Pollard), which demonstrates itself every moment of the day when the objects (she means 'object') of his affection are present with him, in a thousand almost imperceptible attentions to their wishes (she means 'her wishes'), in a sort of restless watchfulness which I know not how to describe." In another letter she declares "he was never tired of comforting his sister, he never left her in anger, he always met her with joy, he preferred her society to every other pleasure, or rather when we were so happy as to be within each other's reach he had no pleasure when we were compelled to be divided". Is not this the lover of whom all girls dream? William speaks for himself: "Oh, my dear, dear sister, with what transport shall I again meet you, with what rapture shall I again wear out the day in your sight. I assure you so eager is my desire to see you that all obstacles vanish. I see you in a moment running or rather flying to my arms."[1]

I have made rather much of this point because I believe the truth of William's "cure" to be that he was not only cured by Dorothy and Coleridge, but to some extent effected his own cure by putting himself into a situation where passionate love could keep his soul in a constant glow of happiness. The happy temperament which in him had been built up in his free youth was native to Dorothy. Speaking of her last *Journal*,

[1] Dr. J. C. Smith sees William's love for Dorothy as just another example of his affection for his family. This is unnecessarily discreet.

written in the years just before her breakdown, Harper says, 'The same happy heart was in her as of old, the same enjoyment of life's never-ending spectacle". So, although there were elements of pain left over from the past few years, love and two happy hearts brought about their assimilation. Some commentators think the assimilation was anything but complete in the Racedown years, on the evidence of the lines in the *Prelude* where Wordsworth tells us that at this period he was

> inwardly oppressed
> With sorrow, disappointment, vexing thoughts,
> Confusion of opinion, zeal decayed,
> And lastly utter loss of hope itself
> And things to hope for.

But in another reference to this same episode he speaks of "the complete composure, and the happiness entire", which were his at Racedown; or, as the 1850 text puts it, "from morn to night, unbroken cheerfulness serene", echoing a sentence of Dorothy's in a letter written from Racedown: "William is as cheerful as anybody can be: perhaps you may not think it, but he is the life of the whole house". Indeed, the letters neither of William nor of Dorothy at this time afford any signs of depression, and we may well suppose that, supported by nature, freedom, and the companionship of Dorothy, William's ingrained happiness was able to take the disturbing elements in its stride.

But Wordsworth's happiness was only based as to one half upon his life with Dorothy and his love for her: it was equally due to his now uncircumscribed choice of poetry as a career. To put it in another way—his happiness could leave the state of passive bliss and become ebullient and creative only when it was directed into the channel for which the purpose of life intended it. The advent of Coleridge doubled, for a period, Wordsworth's happiness, and at the same time inspired it to serve the divine ends of poetry. It was in June 1797, some eighteen months after the Wordsworths came to Racedown, that Coleridge effectively entered their joint life, walking over from Nether Stowey, more than thirty miles away, leaping over the last gate, and bounding down the field to greet his new friends. Wordsworth was just twenty-seven, and had as yet done little to justify his indomitable sense of "the Poet's soul". The coming of Coleridge set something free, and *Lyrical Ballads* followed within a year, the first of a short series of inspired volumes.

The effect on Coleridge of the poetic friendship was hardly less striking. Mrs. Sandford notes that during the year when the Wordsworths were at Alfoxden "Coleridge was in better health and happier in mind than he had almost ever been before, or ever was to be again". Before June 1797 he had to his credit an even smaller output of memorable poetry than Wordsworth; under the stimulus of the new contact he swiftly produced that generous handful of great poems by which alone he takes rank among the gods. Coleridge's inspiration was drawn, like Wordsworth's, from the triune companionship of the two poets and Dorothy, and it is tempting to speculate on what might have been the result of this companionship continuing at the top of its form over a long period. This implies that the Coleridge who leapt into the Wordsworths' life in the summer of 1797 should have been unmarried and free from the curse of opium, so that he and Wordsworth might indeed have been, as the *Prelude* claims hopefully,

> Predestined, if two beings ever were,
> To seek the same delights, to have one health,
> One happiness.

Three major consequences follow upon this supposition, I believe: for Dorothy, health greatly improved (probably the avoidance of the ultimate breakdown), and happiness robbed of infinite pain; for William, the completed *Recluse*; for Coleridge, perhaps a position among English poets second only to Shakespeare.

Of the strange happiness of the "three persons and one soul" which lasted, at Racedown and presently at Alfoxden, for just a year, much has been written; from Wordsworth's angle it is not difficult to understand. Amid scenery of "enchanting beauty", as he himself called it, with the quickening influence of Dorothy's love and Coleridge's admiration and talk, we need not wonder that Dorothy was able to write to Mary, "William's faculties seem to expand every day. He composes with much more facility than he did . . . and his ideas flow faster than he can express them", while William himself told James Losh, "the work of composition is carved out for me for at least a year and a half". No poet would ask for more in Paradise. In the *Prelude* he attributes his happiness mainly to nature still. Coleridge came, he says, to "regulate his soul", Dorothy to "preserve him still a poet";

> And lastly Nature's self, by human love
> Assisted, . . .
> Gave me that strength and knowledge full of peace,
> Enlarged, and never more to be disturbed,
> Which through the steps of our degeneracy,
> All degradation of this age, hath still
> Upheld me, and upholds me at this day.

Presently he points with exactitude to that secret and invulnerable happiness which is the characteristic of the "way":

> in Nature still
> Glorying, I found a counterpoise in her,
> Which, when the spirit of evil was at its height,
> Maintained for me a secret happiness.

Later still he shows, as in many other places, how exquisitely Dorothy played her part of adapting nature to this beneficent end. His own way of approach, he says, was complex and insatiable, "still craving combinations of new forms", but Dorothy,

> wise as women are
> When genial circumstance hath favoured them,
> (She) welcomed what was given, and craved no more.

> Whatever scene was present to her eyes
> That was the best, to that she was attuned
> Through her humility and lowliness
> And through a perfect happiness of soul . . .
> For she was Nature's inmate . . .

And so at length he himself stood, "in Nature's presence, a sensitive and a creative soul".

Something of what he was at the end of this second phase—the first under the new influences—may be seen in the poem he composed at its concluding moment. When, in June 1798, the Wordsworths had to quit Alfoxden, William took Dorothy for a three or four days' walk in the Wye valley, to show her the beauties that had thrilled him on his solitary tramp five years before. The last day of the walk must have been a strange one for his companion, or would have been strange for any companion but Dorothy. For William was hard at work composing a poem. He can hardly have shone, on this day, as a conversationalist, but Dorothy will have listened with content and expectation to the mutterings which were the sign that William's muse was in action,[1] and she got her reward when, on their reaching Bristol, William dictated to her the day's result. The lovely tribute to herself was the first of a long series, and we can imagine her weeping with wonder and delight. It must have made Wordsworth very happy to write the *Tintern Abbey* lines: he said, many years later, "No poem of mine was composed under circumstances more pleasant for me to remember than this".

For himself at this point in his life, the poem shows him as one who had learnt to win tranquil restoration from the exposure of the whole being, body and spirit, to the sunlight of happiness, remembered and regained; one who had achieved the mystic possibility of a serene and blessed mood in which his soul rose above material phenomena, and, by the deep power of joy, pierced through them to the underlying life; one whom the

---

[1] In later days, when Dorothy was writing her occasional verses, she would sit muttering to herself after the approved model.

sublime sense of the interpenetrative presence of God disturbed with the joy of elevated thoughts. The poem marks a considerable advance upon the position at which the poet had stood as he finished with Cambridge, relying for delight on "the ever-living Universe and the independent spirit of pure youth".

The nine months spent in Germany form an unnatural break in the lives of the Wordsworths, if not of Coleridge. William and Dorothy did not like what they saw of either Hamburg or Goslar, and only began to enjoy themselves when they set out to walk south from the latter place. They were parted from Coleridge, who wrote, "William my head and my heart! dear William and dear Dorothea! You have all in each other; but I am lonely and want you!" He told Poole the Wordsworths were "melancholy and hypp'd" at the thought that on returning to England they might not be able to be near him, but Dorothy wrote to Coleridge: "Wherever we finally settle (in the north) you must come to us at the latter end of next summer, and we will explore together every nook of that romantic country. You might walk through Wales and Yorkshire and join us in the county of Durham, and I would follow at your heels and hear your dear voices again." The momentum of Wordsworth's productivity continued, and a letter from Dorothy to Mary Hutchinson gives the first suggestion of his "composition sickness": "William is very industrious, and his mind is always active; indeed too much so, he overwearies himself, and suffers from pain and weakness in the side". However, she told Christopher they had lived "very happily and comfortably", and William said they had passed the time very pleasantly but were glad to be home again—to the third and final phase of creative happiness that his life was to know.

A preliminary but exceedingly valuable eight months were spent at Sockburn, whence Wordsworth and Coleridge, presently joined by John Wordsworth, set out for a walk through the Lakes. One's heart expands to think of those three godlike young men (for, as Coleridge said, John was of the true kin of William and Dorothy) striding over by Hawes Water, Troutbeck, Windermere, Hawkshead, Ambleside, Rydal and Grasmere to the Grisedale Pass, where John parted from them to join his ship. Before he went he and William had discussed the purchase or renting of a house at Grasmere where Dorothy might come to live again with William; William wrote to tell Dorothy of the scheme—"you will think me mad", he said, but Dorothy will have thought it a divine madness. William and Coleridge went on walking and talking for a month or more, and William at least drew from that renewed intimacy sustenance for years of inspired writing. *Lyrical Ballads* had sold badly, and, as Mrs. Coleridge took some pleasure in repeating, "were not liked at all". Yet Southey had grudgingly admitted that every piece discovered genius, and Lamb gloried in both *Tintern Abbey* and *The Ancient Mariner*.

However, at the moment, it was life not literature that was on the move, and in December 1799, after an epic journey through "Wensley's rich dale", over "Sedbergh's naked heights", and by the beauty-haunted Kendal-Keswick road once more, the brother and sister came to the hill-girt home which, with occasional shiftings a mile or two one way or the other, was to be conjointly theirs till death. By happy instinct, or by some intimacy of understanding, they had chosen the very heart of Lakeland for this, their first real home, after the very successful experiments in domesticity in other people's houses. Mileage, measured by the compasses, was of little account to Wordsworth, who preferred to note how the valleys spread out spoke-wise from Scafell and Helvellyn as hubs. But if the geometrical centre of a district is its heart, Grasmere provides a heart for the Lakes. A circle drawn with a radius of fifteen miles from Grasmere includes practically the whole of the Lake District, with all the mountains except High Pike to the north beyond Saddleback and all the lakes except for the western extremity of Ennerdale and the northern half of Bassenthwaite. The roads indeed radiate from Ambleside, but Ambleside is only a step from Grasmere, as Dorothy, who generally walked over for the letters, knew. Wordsworth called the spot a "centre", possibly intending the geometrical sense:

> A termination and a last retreat,
> A centre, come from wheresoe'er you will,
> A whole without dependence or defect,
> Made for itself.

Grasmere to-day is not the sparse and isolated village of 1800, yet, in our less exacting degree, those enthusiastic phrases of Wordsworth's are still applicable. Here was the prospect of half a century of happiness. Why the eventuality ran to only a quarter of that time we shall see.

The poet's anticipations are shown in the opening lines of the great canto, *Home at Grasmere*, which appears to have been composed on a fine morning in February 1800, that is, about two months after the arrival at the cottage. Here, without disguise or qualification, are the very heights of love and happiness. He had loved the fascinating seclusion of the spot as a boy,

> And now 'tis mine, perchance for life, dear Vale!
> Beloved Grasmere (let the wandering Streams
> Take up, the cloud-capt hills repeat, the Name)
> One of thy lowly dwellings is my home.

He admits to having had "apprehensions" about what the "realities of life" might bring him, but now he "blushes for them": they are things of the past, for he is in Grasmere, with Dorothy!

> On Nature's invitation do I come,
> By Reason sanctioned. Can the choice mislead
> That made the calmest, fairest spot on earth,
> With all its unappropriated good,
> My own; and not mine only, for with me . . .
> Under yon orchard, in yon humble cot . . .
> The only daughter of my parents dwells:
> Aye, think on that, my heart, and cease to stir;
> Pause upon that, and let the breathing frame
> No longer breathe, but all be satisfied.

He proceeds to what is perhaps the loveliest of his many appreciations of what Dorothy was to him:

> Mine eyes did ne'er
> Fix on a lovely object, nor my mind
> Take pleasure in the midst of happy thoughts,
> But either she whom now I have, who now
> Divides with me this loved abode, was there
> Or not far off. Where'er my footsteps turned,
> Her voice was like a hidden Bird that sang;
> The thought of her was like a flash of light
> Or an unseen companionship, a breath
> Of fragrance independent of the wind.

So he feels his happiness is such as cannot be excelled:

> The boon is absolute; surpassing grace
> To me hath been vouchsafed; among the bowers
> Of blissful Eden this was neither given
> Nor could be given; possession of the good
> Which had been sighed for, ancient thoughts fulfilled,
> And dear imaginations realised
> Up to the highest measure, yea, and more.

How the vision translated itself may be seen in the *Letters* and in Dorothy's *Journals*. Summarising their activities for Jane, Dorothy wrote that when out of doors they walked, boated, sat, and fished (particularly when John was a visitor), and in the house they talked, wrote and read—though reading had its limitations, for when Wordsworth wrote to Wrangham in January 1801 he said he had not seen a new book since they came thirteen months ago. There were also tea and bonfires on the island in Grasmere lake. They were completely free, charmingly housed in the loveliest surroundings. They were isolated, but what neighbours they had were of the kind their hearts delighted in, and their visitors were again always of the "worthwhile" order. John was with them for months, and they had the extreme pleasure of having Coleridge at Keswick. Greta Hall was indeed fourteen miles away over Dunmail Raise, but that only added to the luminous ecstasy of Dorothy's frequent entry in the *Journal*, "Coleridge came". The most dramatic of these entries is that of August 31, 1800: "At 11 o'clock Coleridge came, when I was walking in the still clear moonshine in the garden. He came over Helvellyn. William was gone to bed, and John also, worn out with his ride round Coniston. We sate and chatted till half past three, William in his dressing-gown. Coleridge read us a part of *Christabel*. Talked much about the mountains etc." Life is high romance when such an incident as this can arise naturally from it. A less heady happiness is felt in other entries: "William sate beside me and read *The Pedlar*. He was in high spirits, and full of hope of what he should do with it". Or again: "When we returned William wasted his time in the Magazines. I wrote to Coleridge and Mrs. C. Then we sate by the fire, and were happy, only our tender thoughts became painful." Dorothy writes to Mary to tell how she and William walked back from Eusemere to Grasmere over Kirkstone: "We sauntered and rested, loved all that we saw, each other, and thee, our dear Mary—sauntered and rested, lounged and were lazy. . . . Dear Mary, we are glad to be at home— No fireside is like this."

The Grasmere Journal goes beyond the bare objectivity of the collection of exquisite prose pieces which Dorothy put together at Alfoxden, and we get an impression of a busy, active, varied life. Unfortunately (as we learn from de Selincourt's complete text, though Knight, the first editor, had carefully suppressed the facts) both Dorothy and William suffered from continuous minor ailments during the first two and a half years at Dove Cottage, and at one point William surprisingly writes, in answer to an invitation to Yorkshire, "I am not strong enough to walk and too poor to ride". Part of the trouble, though not all, was his "composition sickness", the sad complexities of which are described by Dorothy to Jane: "He writes with so much feeling and agitation that it brings on a sense of pain and internal weakness about his left side and stomach, which now often makes it impossible for him to write when he is in mind and feelings in such a state that he could do it without difficulty"—the greater the degree of inspiration the greater the physical obstacle. Nevertheless there is always happiness at the heart of things, and for herself Dorothy says, writing to Mary and Sara, "Really it is almost a pleasure to be ill, William is so good and loving to me".

A joyous aspect of life at Dove Cottage—one which will shock some readers as it evidently shocked Knight, who covered up all traces of it—was the pleasure the poetical brother and sister took in their meals. This is surely a legitimate inference from Dorothy's obvious interest in her cookery and the gusto with which she set down the varied chronicle of their dietary: "Peas for dinner", "Supped upon a hare", "Ate hasty pudding and went to bed", "We had pork to dinner sent us by Mr. Simpson", "We got no dinner but gooseberry pie to our tea", "After tea Mr. Simpson came with large potatoes and plumbs" (Lamb would have liked the collocation as well as the spelling), "I gave William his dinner—a beefsteak", "William and Coleridge sat for some time in the orchard; then they came in to supper—mutton chops and potatoes", and a pleasing one about herself: "I felt myself weak, and William charged me not to go to Mrs. Lloyd's, but when he was gone I thought I would get the visit over if I could, so I ate a beefsteak, thinking it would strengthen me; and so it did, and I had a very pleasant walk".

The days were coloured, some in quieter hues than others. Here are two, a bright one and one in lower tones.

"Sept. 1. 1800. We walked in the wood by the lake. William read *Joanna*, and *The Firgrove*, to Coleridge. They bathed. The morning was delightful, with somewhat of an autumnal freshness. After dinner Coleridge discovered a rock seat in the orchard. Cleared away the brambles. Coleridge obliged to go to bed after tea. John and I followed William up the hill, and then returned to go to Mr. Simpson's. We borrowed bottles for bottling rum. The evening somewhat frosty and grey, but very pleasant. I broiled Coleridge a mutton chop, which he ate in bed. William was gone to bed. I chatted with John and Coleridge till near 12."

"March 23. 1802. A mild morning. William worked at the *Cuckoo* poem. I sewed beside him. After dinner he slept, I read German, and at the closing in of the day went to sit in the orchard—he came to me, and walked backwards and forwards. We talked about Coleridge. William repeated the poem to me. I left him there, and in twenty minutes he came in rather tired with attempting to write. He is now reading Ben Jonson. I am going to read German. It is about ten o'clock, a quiet night. The fire flutters and the watch ticks. I hear nothing else save the breathing of my Beloved, and he now and then pushes his book forward, and turns over a leaf. Fletcher is not come home. No letter from C."

The poetic soul of the life at Dove Cottage at this time is to be seen and felt in the *Castle of Indolence* stanzas, where Wordsworth tells us that they dwelt there, "in our happy Castle"—"from earthly labour free" (though this applies to himself and Coleridge more than to Dorothy!) "as happy spirits as were ever seen".

So pass two years and a half. Then comes the interlude of William's marriage, after which life goes on as before—with a difference. A few days before the wedding, Dorothy wrote from Gallow Hill, Mary's home: "My dear Jane, if this letter reaches you before next Monday you will think of me travelling towards our own dear Grasmere with my most beloved Brother and his wife. I have long loved Mary Hutchinson as a sister, and she is equally attached to me; this being so, you will guess that I look forward with perfect happiness to this connection between us, but, happy as I am, I half dread that concentration of all tender feelings, past, present and future, which will come upon me on the wedding morning. There never lived on earth a better woman than Mary H., and I have not a doubt but that she is in every respect formed to make an excellent wife for my Brother, and I seem myself to have scarcely anything left to wish for but that the wedding was over, and we had reached our home again." It is impossible to read those sentences without hearing in their brave lucidity a note of dread, perhaps a note of doom. William's marriage to Mary Hutchinson for a time increased his happiness, and introduced permanently into his life a strain of happiness of a commonplace kind. It brought, too, a new happiness to Dorothy. But the happiness which was her very self was shattered by this marriage: it had not even been cracked by the *affaire Annette*. She held her shattered happiness together with the steady hand of unselfish love, and no one but William ever guessed that it was not whole as before. But William knew, and the knowledge that that unique happiness and that supreme love had been betrayed cankered his own happiness. Doubtless the betrayal was forced upon William, but I do not think it was planned so far ahead as is sometimes supposed. On the somewhat tepid evidence of an early MS. poem written in part translation part imitation of a Horatian Ode, de Selincourt says that when Wordsworth chose Dove Cottage for himself and Dorothy he had already prospected such a retreat in that spot for himself and Mary Hutchinson. In the poem, *Home at Grasmere*, when Wordsworth describes his sensations and thoughts as he looks down on Dove Cottage from one of the neighbouring heights he makes no reference to Mary, except as one of several "sisters of our hearts" who are to visit him and Dorothy. Having told of sailor John's sojourn at the Cottage, he goes on to speak of his expectation that

> others whom we love
> Will seek us also, Sisters of our hearts,
> And one, like them, a Brother of our hearts,
> Philosopher and Poet, in whose sight
> These mountains will rejoice with open joy.

But there is not the slightest sign that he was in any sense looking forward at that time to bringing a wife to share Dove Cottage.

There are some who, seeing a canker at the heart of Wordsworth's happiness after 1802, attribute it to remorse for the amour with Annette. There is no evidence for any such remorse, and Wordsworth's handling of the situation points to anything but a divided mind: it was firm almost to callousness. His solution was to marry Mary Hutchinson, thus not only terminating (or reducing to a social item) the connection with Annette, but (what was of far greater human importance) deposing Dorothy from her rightful position as his inspiration, his beloved, his companion and his slave. I sometimes think it would have been better had he made with Annette the *mariage de convenance* which Annette probably supposed the marriage with Mary to be, leaving Dorothy in possession of her spiritual kingdom, and Mary to marry John. This idyll is built on a number of doubtful assumptions, including the assumption that Annette was considerably less irrelevant to the Wordsworth design for living than she apparently was; but however bizarre the *ménage*, its central figure would have been a poet true to himself—or to the unique life-idea represented by himself and Dorothy. But it is not likely that Wordsworth felt anything, or much, of this. His egoism (the backbone of his poetry) prevented him from realising any one of the several disloyalties comprehended in the one error. Yet he knew, "in the last place of refuge, his own soul", that an aspect of death had fallen over Dorothy's bright joy.

It is with some compunction that I, who am all for marriage, and believe it to be the supreme human relation, find myself appearing to disparage Mary Hutchinson and her marriage with William Wordsworth. But once caught by the spell of Dorothy's personality, by the beauty of her strange love, by the pitifulness of her absorption in Mary's home, by the tragedy of her multiple frustrations—you are helpless, and can but feel a fiery resentment against both William and Mary for their dimming of the light of that rare and lovely life. Dorothy's sacrifice pleases those who find pleasure in contemplating such painful things, but its net result was an appalling diminution in the sum total of happiness, and it ought never to have been made—never to have been demanded of her. All life is lovelier by reason of what Dorothy Wordsworth was at Racedown, at Alfoxden, and during the first few years at Dove Cottage; it is but sadder for what she was afterwards.

Outwardly life went on very much as before: the current of life at Dove Cottage was too strong to be deflected by the taking in of so sympathetic a personality as Mary's. Coleridge comes and goes, and William and Dorothy are still two halves of a perfect whole. The *Journal* continues long enough to give us this picture of Christmas Eve 1802: "William is now sitting by me, at ½ past 10 o'clock. I have been beside him ever since tea, running the heel of a stocking, repeating some of his sonnets to him, listening to his own repeating, reading some of Milton's, and the *Allegro* and *Penseroso*. It is a quiet keen frost. Mary is in the parlour below attending to the baking of cakes, and Jenny Fletcher's pies. Sara is in bed with the toothache. Mary is well and I am well and Molly is as blithe as last year at this time. Coleridge came this morning with Wedgwood. We all turned out of William's bedroom one by one to meet him. He looked well."

But presently she says, "It is to-day Christmas Day, Saturday 25 of December 1802. I am 31 years of age. It is a dull frosty day . . ." and then, after a fortnight, "Again I have neglected to write my Journal"; and a few days after that she gave up the effort—the *Journal* trickles out. Something had happened to the source of the crystal flow.

Celestial happiness of the spirit such as Dorothy had known for the past seven years cannot perhaps be expected to last longer than some such period. Yet in her case—so long and patient had been her waiting, so faultless her bearing under the great duty and privilege of happiness—we are allowed to feel that her allotment might well have been trebled without putting any undue strain upon the scheme of things. *Dis aliter visum*. Her happiness with William was withered at the root. True, another tree of happiness grew up in its place. But it was no fairy tree now, no golden-apple tree of the Hesperides; the apples it bore were of a sound culinary variety. Domesticity can be a lovely thing, if it is kept in its place: it usurped a tyrannical function when it was allowed to submerge the gipsy Dorothy. Babies are often charming, and always hopeful: Dorothy's obsession with the successive offspring of William and Mary calls to mind (if distantly) the painful metamorphosis of Natasha at the end of *War and Peace*. This is not to deny that her love for the children was abundantly beautiful. Little John was but eleven days old when Dorothy began to rhapsodise upon him, ". . . how happy we are with this blessed Infant—his noble countenance—his fine head—his beautiful nose"; later on his violent passions and angry squalls occasion reverential comment. And so with Dora, though as Dora was a girl and not the first-born Dorothy's love did not now preclude criticism. As the children grew up she became Aunt Dorothy: universally beloved and respected, but Dorothy Wordsworth is now Aunt Dorothy. With Mary her relations were perfect: there is no evidence to the contrary, and only a little evidence that perfection was preserved at a certain cost.

It is William's happiness, not Dorothy's, that is my theme; but William and Dorothy were one spiritual being, and everything that happened to Dorothy happened to William. Coleridge was happening to them both. The deterioration in his health, complicated by his indulgence in opium, was making him a difficult friend, but they knew the infinite value of his personality and their love was unimpaired. Shortly after the birth of William's first child, the three went off on a six weeks' tour of Scotland, thinking to recapture the thrills of the expeditions from Alfoxden and Nether Stowey. But this time, in place of the magic formula by which Coleridge had evaluated the triple relationship in those carefree days, the group comprised three persons and one horse; and after a fortnight it broke up under circumstances which might have left unpleasant feelings in minds whose reciprocal disposition was less generous. William and Dorothy continued their tour in circumstances of much physical discomfort but measureless spiritual delight. As Dorothy wrote afterwards, "We were very happy during our tour, particularly the last month—the rambling disposition came upon us". (She would have loved Dr. Lin Yu Tang's idea of travel —"wandering farther and farther happy of heart".) Harper says well, "The annoyances and distractions of travel affected them little. Every sunrise was to them the beginning of an adventure, a new life, like the dawn of a child's holiday. It is hardly too much to say that nothing commonplace happened to them during those six weeks. If the sky was blue, that was a miracle; if rain fell and ways were foul, that was wonderful too."

Though they continued to regard Coleridge with passionate affection, the parting in Scotland dealt the friendship a jarring blow from which it never completely recovered. During the succeeding months they saw him chiefly in the throes of appalling illness, part of it endured at Dove Cottage, where he gave Mary and Dorothy an incredible amount of trouble. With William there were theological disputes which caused acrimonious reproaches on Coleridge's part, for he was already sunk deep in a sentimental orthodoxy, and though Wordsworth was proceeding to a like end it was on much more deliberate and rational lines. Then came Coleridge's absence abroad, lasting for nearly two and a half years, during which his correspondence and neglect of correspondence were maddening. At length he came back to them—physically so changed as to shock his best friends. But though there was pain there was no diminution in their love, and it was in January 1807, while they were all staying at Coleorton, that Wordsworth read to Coleridge the completed *Prelude*, which at this time had no other name than "the poem to Coleridge". The incident of the reading is more deeply interesting than almost anything comparable in the history of English literature: Coleridge's thoughts as he listened—both those he put into the poem he wrote afterwards and those others that can be imagined—have an almost unbearable poignancy. Followed the trying, despairful, long-drawn-out, episode of the editing of *The Friend* from Allan Bank: a sense of pathos blended of tragic hope and joyless romance still possesses the room where Coleridge and Sara worked. And then, like the foreseen and inevitable end of an Elizabethan tragedy, came the embittered, futile quarrel between Wordsworth and Coleridge at the end of 1810. It was years since Wordsworth had ceased to draw inspiration from his friend: now the stream of friendship itself, which had grown more and more slender but had never dried up, was lost in bogs and sands (though love and admiration remained on both sides), and a second essential element in Wordsworth's happiness was dead.

The years during which the two elements—those connected with Coleridge and with Dorothy—had been slowly losing their vital warmth present a picture manifestly less bright than that of the preceding period. Writing to Wrangham in 1804, Wordsworth says, "I have a son, and a noble one too he is as ever was seen. He is a great comfort and pleasure to us in this lonely place. My sister continues to live with me. I read, walk, doze a little in the afternoon, and live upon the whole what you may call a tolerably rational life, I mean as the world goes." It may be doubted whether he would ever have thought of calling the Cottage lonely, or of describing its inhabitants as needing to be comforted, in the days when he lived there with Dorothy; and the rest of the letter has a similar faint tone of disillusion. The old exhilarating belief in man is beginning to be replaced by a fear of social and religious change. The patronage of Sir George Beaumont creeps insidiously in. The strange but not undignified "composition sickness" now takes the form of an almost unbelievable complication of pains which seizes him whenever he takes up a pen to write a letter.

Death played its part, not at first a part that needed to be fatal to happiness. The death of John Wordsworth in February 1805 had beauty as well as sorrow in it, and William and Dorothy's strength of happiness was sufficient to stand up to the affliction, grievous as it was. In the letters of the ensuing eight months we can watch the gradual healing of Dorothy's wounded soul, and when in November she and William got off together on a few days' "wander" round Ullswater she was able to record, "We were as happy travellers as ever paced side by side in a holiday ramble". We may be sure that William's soul was convalescent too, and seven years after John's death he dared to describe himself as one of the happiest of men. But now death fell in far more dreadful form. Just a month after Wordsworth's proud claim, chronicled by Crabb Robinson on May 8, 1812, the darling child Catherine died, to be followed before the end of the year by the beloved little Thomas. Back in 1800, when Wordsworth had spoken of "a never failing principle of joy" in which he had "a faith that fails not in all sorrow", he might have recovered even from these blows, but now his state was such that happiness went out like a blown candle. The progress of events during the past decade had "deprived [him] of *courage*, in the sense the word bears when applied by Chaucer to the animation of birds". It was nearly twenty years later that he used these words about himself, but they are true in some degree of the whole period after 1812, and towards its close, in 1846, he permitted himself to say, "I often think that my life has been in a great measure wasted". One can only feel glad that Dorothy was not in a condition to be aware of that expression of disloyalty to all that he and she had been in their great days.

The happiness which slowly failed during the decade previous to 1812, and which I have described as "going out" in that year, was happiness in the sense in which it is used throughout this book: happiness as a fire in the soul, a nightingale in the heart—a living creed and a creative force, a way of life and the spirit of religion. That lesser kind of happiness which means cheerful spirits came presently back, and left Wordsworth, on Miss Batho's beautifully accumulated evidence, as delightful a a figure, to all who were not unworthy of the relation, as any elderly lion that ever growled. Let Sara Coleridge, writing to Quillinan when the poet lay dying, corroborate the story: "He used to be so glad, so cheerful and happy-minded. No mind could be more sufficient to itself, teeming with matter of delight, fresh gushing founts rising up perpetually in the region of the imagination. . . . No mind was ever richer within itself, and more abundant in material of happiness, independent of chance or change, save such as affected the mind itself." Since Sara Coleridge was a girl of twenty in 1812, this beautiful tribute must apply at least partly to the latter part of Wordsworth's life. Nor must we forget what Blake told us: that we go safely through life only if we keep in mind that joy and woe are woven fine: the two are not to be separated: happiness, or unhappiness, once experienced is for ever part of life. The unhappiness (or lower order of happiness) of the latter half of Wordsworth's life does not cancel out the intense happiness of the first half. He had experienced happiness to the full, and penetrated its mystery in the light of poetry as no other English writer has done. The poetic penetration I shall examine further in later chapters. That he had once held the living creed of creative happiness may be judged from his enunciation of its terms as he entered upon his kingdom. Knowing, as few have known better, what it was to be a poet, he thus, in the Preface to *Lyrical Ballads*, defined the poet: "A poet is a man who rejoices more than other men in the spirit of life that is in him, who looks at the world in the spirit of love, acknowledging the beauty of the universe, and paying homage to the grand elementary principle of pleasure by which he knows, and feels, and lives, and moves".

CHAPTER III

Poetry along the Way

FROM THE southern shore of Rydal Mere one looks across the water to Wordsworth's Walk—the "far terrace", as the family at the Mount used to call it. I sometimes think I see him still pacing there, waiting, like the Scholar Gipsy, for the spark from heaven to fall—the spark that should light up *The Recluse*. With Milton's blindness and Beethoven's deafness must be placed the failure of Wordsworth's inspiration, a failure which evinced itself in many ways, but is seen most tragically in the uncompleted *Recluse*. Everyone knows the grandiose scheme which Wordsworth outlined, for a philosophical poem in three parts, to be called *The Recluse*: the *Prelude* to be introductory to this great tripartite poem, and the rest of his poetic output to constitute a series of annotations or illustrative sidelights. Everyone knows, too, that *The Excursion*, composed steadily between 1801 and 1811, was intended as the second part of *The Recluse*, and that Part III was never written. What are not so generally realised are the facts concerning Part I: how, very soon after he and Dorothy settled at Dove Cottage, Wordsworth took pen in hand and, with what exalted hope, headed a manuscript page:

THE RECLUSE

PART FIRST

Book First — Home at Grasmere

—proceeding to compose, under this inscription, the lovely lines, some 900 in all, beginning,

A boy stood looking into Grasmere Vale,

and ending with the great "fragment" which is all that is generally printed (and which may have been composed earlier). Then inspiration failed—along that particular line. True, he switched over to Part II, and by years of faithful labour consummated that glorious achievement, *The Excursion*. But Wordsworth went on writing verse for thirty-six years after *The Excursion* was published. Many times, in the early part of this period, Dorothy writes joyfully to someone that William is busy with "his great poem"—busy thinking about it, she must have meant, for no results of the busy-ness have been preserved. Later she changes her note—William cannot be persuaded to get down to the *magnum opus*. Coleridge lends his ineffectual urging, but there is a dead hand over William. *The Recluse, Part First, Book I*, stands as a solitary canto.

De Selincourt suggests that Wordsworth used up too much material in writing the *Prelude*, but I for one get the impression that under the proper stimulus the contents and creativity of Wordsworth's mind were inexhaustible. But the stimulus was gone: Coleridge was ill and increasingly estranged, Dorothy submerged in household cares; and happiness, the fountain-light of all his day, burning low and presently extinguished. And perhaps as he entered middle age—with five ailing children (two of them, by 1812, dead), in crowded, damp and smoky quarters exchanged only for the comforts of officialdom—the high dream enshrined in that significant title spoke to him in tones too bitterly ironic.

Nevertheless, Wordsworth had known happiness as few poets have known it. The happiness which was his in his youth and in the Coleridge-Dorothy years provided inspiration for ten years' output of poetry which, in depth, height, and quality of spiritual vision, is with difficulty paralleled. It was not altogether Wordsworth's fault if after that the radiance faded into the light of common day; but as the inspiration of happiness died the visionary power died too. I suppose the question of the dying out of poetic power is an agreed one: and yet only the other day a noted publicist spoke casually of "the later and greater poems of Wordsworth". This is either perversity or sheer lack of critical sense. It is hardly possible that by "later" poems the writer meant *The White Doe of Rylstone*, composed in 1807 and 1808, and *The Excursion*, which was mainly written earlier but was finished and revised in the years 1810–13. These are indeed "great", but not "late". Up to 1820 the only "later" poems of notable æsthetic value are the *Duddon Sonnets*, which, considered as a sequence, are admirable, and include, in the *Afterthought*, one of Wordsworth's greatest sonnets; the lines on *The Pass of Kirkstone*; and *Characteristics of a Child Three Years Old*. None of these, except the *Afterthought*, distantly approaches the best of the 1798–1807 poems. After 1820 varying degrees of high quality are found in four or five more sonnets (*Mutability* and *King's College Chapel* from the *Ecclesiastical Sonnets*, "A trouble not of clouds or weeping rain", "Scorn not the sonnet", and "Most sweet it is"), *The Primrose of the Rock*, "If thou indeed derive thy light", *The Skylark*, and the lines on the *Death of James Hogg* (but *not* those on the death of Charles Lamb). Here again there is little that is not dwarfed by any fair sample from the *Lyrical Ballads*. The great bulk of critical opinion agrees in speaking of "the supreme decade", 1798–1807 or 1808. The latter year includes *The White Doe of Rylstone*. I feel the period must be extended to 1811, to allow for the completion of *The Excursion*.

The years during which Wordsworth knew happiness not only in its most intense and exalted form but also in the self-conscious form which alone could be directly useful to his creative imagination were those from September 1795, when the Racedown adventure was initiated, to 1803, the year following his marriage, the year of the Scottish tour. During that period of eight years threequarters of the most inspired of the shorter poems were written; it gave us the great first canto of *The Recluse* and the first part of the *Immortality Ode*; it saw the conception of the *Prelude* and the composition of the first three books, the conception and first two books of *The Excursion*.[1]

---

[1] It is usual to consider this period as terminating in 1805, the year of John Wordsworth's death, but the forces which gradually smothered Wordsworth's happiness were of a less heroic kind than the grief caused by this tragic loss, and they had begun to work before 1805.

Poetic production during the years 1804–8 was still ample, but that of highest quality showed a marked diminishing from the flow of the previous period. It was temporarily interrupted, but not changed in quality, by the death of John. After three months of stunned silence Wordsworth was able to go on and complete the *Prelude*, as de Selincourt points out, in the spirit in which it had been begun: it was in the revisions of twenty and thirty years later that he went back on the "religion of joy" out of which the original poem grew. This period, 1804–8, produced, besides Books IV to XIII of the *Prelude*, most of the remaining quarter of the supreme lyrics, and finally *The White Doe*. During the next three years shades of the prison-house crept closer round the poet, but *The Excursion* was finished before the deaths of the two children came to crush him under a leaden weight of misery. From this time, though his years were but forty-two, he was mentally an old man, shrinkingly afraid of life; charming to his many devoted friends, cantankerous to people who pestered; an adored and adoring, indulgent and tyrannical father, who told Miss Fenwick in 1844 that he "deemed it fit and right" that his daughter Dora, "acting as she has chosen to do (i.e. marrying Quillinan) with my strongest disapprobation", should be "somewhat straitened"; a good husband who found it necessary to apologise to his wife for exhibitions of harsh temper; the only unbroken links with his earlier self his worship of nature and the inviolable though now inoperative bond with Dorothy. During the same period he was a poet of great industry and technical capacity, but of only occasional inspiration.

Thus poetry synchronised with happiness. It had also, as we have noticed, a clear time-relation with Coleridge. When S.T.C. paid his first visit to Racedown Wordsworth was twenty-seven, an age at which Shelley had written *Alastor*, *The Revolt of Islam*, and the *West Wind Ode*; Byron had written *English Bards and Scotch Reviewers* and most of *Childe Harold*; Keats had completed his marvellous production and gone to pledge the Mermaid in the Zodiac; and Milton had written *L'Allegro*, *Il Penseroso* and *Comus*; though to be sure Shakespeare had but shown a dazzling promise in the two long poems and a couple of minor plays. Wordsworth, in June 1797, was known as the author of *An Evening Walk, Descriptive Sketches, Guilt and Sorrow* and *The Borderers*, none of which would have given him a much better claim to immortality than the sheaf of juvenilia for which he was also responsible. Yet we are not able to say that Coleridge made Wordsworth a poet (though he possibly made him a lyric poet), for he had also written the "preamble" to the (as yet undreamed of) *Prelude*, and some 400 lines of *The Ruined Cottage*, the fruit of the past year and a half, read to Coleridge on the occasion of his first visit, and afterwards made the nucleus of the first Book of *The Excursion*. There was much here that might rightly rouse Coleridge's enthusiasm, though only the *Prelude* lines, which he was not to hear for ten years yet, proclaim the voice of a new evangelist. Apart from these lines, the chronicle leaves an impression of labour, of slow and painful delivery; there is no sign of that genius for new and lovely verse-measures, and little of that mastery of rhythmic form, which this poet was soon to display; and against the brilliant happiness of the "preamble" there is a grievous majority of didactic seriousness and brooding melancholy. Above all, outside the "preamble" and some touches in the *Cottage* and the *Borderers*, there was little to show that the new poet was not using old and alien methods of contact with the reality which is the poet's material. But Coleridge's fascinated interest in Wordsworth's spiritual processes and his admiration for the results opened Wordsworth's eyes to the fact that his creative mind, his poetic sensibility, were in themselves the one reliable means to the interpretation of life, the knowledge of reality. This came to give, as it were, expert confirmation to what Dorothy had already done for him—"she gave me eyes, she gave me ears, a heart...." At once it is as if the rock has been struck by a prophet—the waters gush forth: lyrics perfect in form and utterance, blank verse as masterly as almost anything in the language, and everywhere the pure Wordsworthian logos: *Early Spring* and *To My Sister*, *Expostulation and Reply* and *The Tables Turned*, *Simon Lee* and *Peter Bell*, *The Thorn* and *The Idiot Boy* and *We are Seven*, *Tintern Abbey* and *The Old Cumber-*

land Beggar and *There was a Boy*. The period of greatest production of supreme poetry thus begun continues and coincides with six years of intimacy between the two poets which followed the meeting at Racedown and ended with the ill-starred Scottish tour in August 1803. The period falls into three divisions. The first, that connected with Racedown and Alfoxden, from June 1797 to June 1798, found its flower in the *Lyrical Ballads* years —1798, 1799, 1800. The month the poets spent together in October 1799 was followed by the *Recluse* canto and Books I–III of the *Prelude*. The best Greta Hall–Dove Cottage years, 1800–3, resulted in the rich lyric productivity of 1802–6, together with the beginning of *The Excursion* and the completion of the *Prelude*. After this, as the poets drew painfully apart, the Coleridge stimulus (which Wordsworth was the first to acknowledge) lost its power, and Wordsworth's genius functioned less and less freely. His belief, expressed in 1806, that some conversation with Coleridge would enable him to "get on swimmingly with *The Recluse*", was not realised, but Coleridge's return to England in that year and his contacts with Wordsworth at Coleorton in 1807 and at Allan Bank in the years 1808–10 may be seen in relation to the writing of *The White Doe* in 1807 and 1808 and the completion of *The Excursion* in the next three years. Soon after the calamitous break with Coleridge in 1810 the stream of great poetry dried up, though we have seen that there were contributory reasons for the cessation of the flow. It is strange that the Coleridge period should have run so exactly with the years of creative happiness, but our consideration, in the last chapter, of Wordsworth's life during those years should have made it plain that Coleridge was only one among the creative forces—the specialised or technical factor.

A theory of Wordsworth's poetry flatly opposed to that which I have been putting forward is sometimes maintained. It takes either of two forms: that Wordsworth cannot stand with the great "tragic" poets because he "ignored the fact of evil"; or that his "profoundest poetry came out of the dark depths of his experience". The former aspect of this criticism is pressed even by sympathetic interpreters of his poetry like Oliver Elton and Catherine Maclean. All they mean by "ignoring the fact of evil" is that the fact of evil had not the same effect on Wordsworth as it has on them; the comparison with the "great tragic poets" is based on the assumption that tragic art is necessarily, and by reason of its tragic content, the only supremely great kind, a notion that is sufficiently disposed of by Chaucer in poetry and Mozart in music. And as it happens, the answer to this disparagement of Wordsworth was given years ago by Walter Raleigh: "Pain and evil, as Wordsworth saw them, did not shake his faith in the law of happiness. Without happiness for its background, tragedy is inconceivable. Wordsworth's view of the world is a complement to that of the tragic poets—he calls attention to the neglected background."

It is not as if Wordsworth had no experience of the tragic side of life. During the first thirty-five years of his life he laid down vast stores of happiness, but in the midst of that period he had sounded the depths of anguish and despair, and from 1805 onwards his resources were tried with a severity that few of the "tragic poets" can have known. As the years wore on, sorrow and fear and the spectacle of evil did have upon Wordsworth something of the depressing effect which is apparently thought to be desirable. But the poetry of 1798 to 1811 (or even that of 1798 to 1800) shows not that Wordsworth "ignored the fact of evil" (did the critics never read *The Thorn*!) but that he assimilated it. At one point he appears to suggest that the evils of life are mistakenly so called. Having spoken of "the realities of life" as "cold and cowardly, ready to betray, stinted in the measure of their grace", he unexpectedly adds, "as we pronounce them, doing them much wrong". But assimilation not denial was his true line. Hear him in the *Prelude*:

> Dust as we are, the immortal spirit grows
> Like harmony in music; there is a dark
> Inscrutable workmanship that reconciles
> Discordant elements, and makes them move
> In one society. How strange that all
> The terrors, pains, and early miseries,

THE WAY OF HAPPINESS

> Regrets, vexations, lassitudes interfused
> Within my mind, should e'er have borne a part,
> And that a needful part, in making up
> The calm existence that is mine when I
> Am worthy of myself!

"Calm existence" does not quite adequately describe the period of active and often ebullient happiness in which this passage was written, but it is important to notice that in so far as his state of mind was blended of terrors, pains, etc., these were of a bearable, educative order, unlike the life-numbing sorrows which came later.

To refute the assertion that Wordsworth's profoundest poetry came out of the "dark depths" of his experience would be to repeat my argument. I might put it with a slight difference by observing that nine-tenths of his profoundest (though I prefer to call it "highest") poetry is to be found in the *Prelude*, *The Excursion*, *Book I of the Recluse*, the *Immortality Ode*, and the two groups of shorter poems placed by Wordsworth under the headings, *Poems of the Imagination* and *Poems of Sentiment and Reflection*; and that most of the poetry comprised under these titles springs from rich and joyous, exalted and happy experience. There are "dark" areas here as elsewhere, of course, for Wordsworth had a sensitive poet's share of tragic knowledge, and possessed, as he more than once says, "two natures". The "darker" one has been made too much of. Coleridge runs the word "hypochondriac" to death in his references to Wordsworth, and talks, in a letter to Poole, of his "hurtfully segregating and isolating his being". The wealth of love and friendship in his life hardly bears this out. "Doubtless", Coleridge adds, "his delights are more deep and sublime, but he has likewise more hours that prey on his flesh and blood." I feel that the "delights more deep and sublime" are very much more significant than the "preying hours". The *Prelude* indicates that it is these latter that are to be regarded as aberrations from the settled way:

> The Poet, gentle creature as he is,
> Hath, like the Lover, his unruly times—

times when the meditative mind is goaded in troubled passion through the groves of life, passion which, says the poet, "I blame no otherwise than as it lasts too long".

Thus, when the greater happiness went out of Wordsworth's life and resilience out of his spirit, absolute poetry went out of his production; and this was when he was not much over forty. It is worth noting that with other poets also the fourth decade has been the last of high achievement. Spenser, Tennyson and Browning all saw the major inspiration cease soon after they had turned forty, and Arnold well before that age. On the other side, Shakespeare's curve of inspiration showed no signs of falling when he deliberately laid down his pen at forty-seven; Cowper found new inspiration in Lady Austen for *The Task* at fifty; Chaucer discovered his greatest theme in the early fifties; Milton, with calm assurance, delayed setting his hand to his supreme work till his sixth decade was well under way.[1] So that if any general law emerges it is that the time when the arteries begin to harden is a critical moment for poetic inspiration: it can be easily killed, or allowed to die, at that stage, but it is equally open to the impulse of new life. In Wordsworth's case no new impulse came, and the destructive agencies were all too effective.

. . . . .

I said in an earlier chapter that the poetry of 1798–1811 "reaches its peaks of achievement when happiness is its theme or its inspiration". In case the assertion may seem to need to be substantiated, those "peaks" are here named (in chronological order of composition), the poems which support the statement being italicised, while those which militate against it are enclosed in brackets:

---

[1] I cannot forbear to add to these names that of Walter de la Mare, whose volume of great and lovely poetry, *The Burning-Glass*, published when the poet was seventy-two, surely constitutes one of the miracles of literature.

THE WAY OF HAPPINESS

(The Thorn)
Lines Written in Early Spring
To My Sister
Expostulation and Reply
The Tables Turned
The Old Cumberland Beggar
Tintern Abbey Lines
There was a Boy
Influence of Natural Objects
The Lucy Poems
Lucy Gray
The Simplon Pass
On Nature's Invitation do I Come
Hartleap Well
(Michael)
Poems on the Naming of Places (most)
The Recluse, Book I
Resolution and Independence

The Cuckoo
Toussaint sonnet
Milton sonnet
"*It is not to be thought of*" sonnet
The Green Linnet
Yew Trees
Solitary Reaper
Yarrow Unvisited
She was a Phantom
Daffodils
(The affliction of Margaret)
The Prelude
(Ode to Duty)
The Waggoner
Immortality Ode
The Happy Warrior
Two Voices sonnet
The White Doe of Rylstone
The Excursion

A few words of explanation or comment seem to be called for. The theme of *Hartleap Well* is melancholy, but it is treated in a mood of tranquil happiness. Of the *Prelude*, the best (most poetical) books are the happy books (those showing the greatest knowledge of happiness)—I, II, IV, V (latter part), VI, XI, XII, XIII (1805 numbering). The story of *The White Doe* is desperately tragic, yet it is made to lead deliberately to a beautiful and happy conclusion. Of the deep happiness of *The Excursion* I have spoken. There remains the great *Ode*. The sombre tone of this poem has been attributed to its having been composed, for the greater part, under the stress of John Wordsworth's death; but de Selincourt has shown that it was probably completed in 1804—and the poem is not, in fact, a sad one. Its gist may be given thus: "On this sweet May morning all nature is happy, and I am happy with nature. But I feel that the freshness of youth's vision has left me. Why is this? It is because as children we are close to God (or immortality, or infinity), but we grow away from Him with the years. Yet we can remember the feelings of our childhood, and can live by the light of the mystic knowledge we then had but could not use. And though the peculiar delight of youth is gone, a wider, deeper, more sensitive happiness comes in later years."[1]

[1] Herford's admirable critique of the *Ode* (*Wordsworth*, pp. 156–163) omits to note that it is more usual for mystic intimations to come not in childhood but in later life.

CHAPTER IV

Some Studies of the Way

i. Love

IT IS A curious thing that the imaginative mind tends to group things in threes (is this due not so much to the pressure of form as to an instinctive desire to avoid grouping in twos, which almost inevitably means finding pairs of opposites, and the imaginative mind prefers agreement to opposition?), and the poets who have gone deepest invariably include love in the triad of life. Faith, hope and love—love greatest of all, said St. Paul, who is not out of place among the poets. Writing for a later age Wordsworth substituted for faith that hardly less powerful incentive to fine living, admiration: "We live by admiration, hope and love". H. L. Simpson, one of the poets who fell frustrated in the Great War, brought in beauty and seasoned the mixture with humour:

> There are three things of worth;
> Let me say this much before all ends:
> Loveliness, and mirth,
> These, and friends.

Loveliness, laughter, and love: a choice as gallant as the soul of the young soldier-poet who made it. Shelley grows ethereal with "light and love and immortality", and brings the same note into politics, making the thronged nations cry aloud, "As with one voice, 'Truth, Liberty, and Love'". Walter de la Mare at last enlarges the ground to include by name what the others imply as their end: he gives us "love, beauty and happiness". Love is fundamental, but happiness is ultimate. To it we must come, and we shall come to it if love is sure. Joy and love and life are separated only at the cost that attends the tearing apart of living tissue.

I have already suggested that the soul of the Wordsworthian happiness is a certain "blind" or "diffusive" love: a love universal as the sun, making no distinction of distant or near, friend or enemy, good or bad, which pours forth from us at moments when we are perfectly happy, and is only on analysis distinguishable from happiness itself; the grand elementary principle of pleasure, a condition worth more than all the wealth and power the world can give; a state in which you love not only God and man but the very stones of the stony path beneath your feet. Save only that it is rare, this love is as creative as the love-passion between man and woman. When Wordsworth, at Cambridge, began daringly to think he might leave some monument behind him, he adds that though he did nothing at the moment he set about accumulating the material of poetry; and how did he do this?—

> I loved, and I enjoyed, that was my chief
> And ruling business, happy in the strength
> And loveliness of imagery and thought.

This is the peasant Michael's "blind love" in more exalted guise. Contrasting it with the "love of one", the last book of the *Prelude* calls it

> a love that comes into the heart
> With awe and a diffusive sentiment;
> Thy love is human merely; this proceeds
> More from the brooding soul, and is divine.

It is of this divine creative love that Wordsworth says,

> By love, for here
> Do we begin and end, all grandeur comes,
> All truth and beauty, from pervading love;
> That gone, we are as dust;

filling in the detail of Goethe's declaration, "Life is love",

which the Wanderer strengthened to "Life is energy of love".
And such love is, or brings, happiness in its most unquestionable form. It brimmed Wordsworth's heart on his return to Esthwaite vale on his first vacation from Cambridge; and when, at the close of the first day, he set out to make "once more the circuit of our little lake", he knew "consummate happiness".

"Blind love" is impersonal in its object but not in its origin. Wordsworth suggests an origin partly human when he shows us a combination of "the common haunts of the green earth" and "the ordinary human interests which they embosom" fastening insensibly on the heart,

> So that we love, not knowing that we love,
> And feel, not knowing whence our feeling comes.

It has, in fact, many sources, and, like the happiness of soul with which it is so nearly identified, it is seldom complete in the absence of a more narrowly human origin, the personal passion of man and woman. Wordsworth was not, in the normal sense, a great love poet, and this perhaps because, between Dorothy, Mary, Annette and "Lucy", his erotic experience could not have that directness, that "simple, sensuous and passionate" quality, necessary to love poetry as to other kinds. Harper says Wordsworth did not trust himself to describe the effect of the passion of love, knowing the intensity of his own nature and fearing the result of any slackening of self-control. Whether this be so or not (and it seems to me an unlikely argument), there is no doubt that sexual love has little place in Wordsworth's poetry, and where present is sublimated. Mary and Annette seem to have played a negligible part in feeding the flame of his inspiration, "Lucy", whether dream-love or real child, a part that was important but limited. The most passionate personal love of his life was his love for Dorothy, and the *Prelude* and the *Recluse* canto show how strongly his happiness, his joyous love of life, and his poetic force were stimulated by his love for her of whom the thought was like a flash of light, a breath of fragrance. Even when in the noble "conclusion" to the *Prelude* he is describing the blind diffusive love growing more intellectual through the aid of imagination, he associates the development, in his own case, with the part played in his life by the "sister of his soul". With this great love ever glowing in his heart he was safe from over-valuing pure reason. Love is to grow intellectual, but it is to remain love: intellect must ascend to the height of *"feeling* intellect". The heart even of the greatest imaginative poet is to be tender, of female softness, full

> Of little loves and delicate desires,
> Mild interests and gentlest sympathies.

Just as Coleridge had declared, "Love is the very air of my genius", so Wordsworth asks, in a letter to Sir George Beaumont, "the thoughts, feelings and images on which the life of my poems depends . . . what have they to do with a life without love?" "Life," exclaims the Pastor, "is love and immortality." Love to Wordsworth, when he wrote the *Prelude*, meant primarily love of life, next the love between himself and Dorothy and then love of mankind. This third species of earthly love is one from which even more unhappiness than happiness can spring. Wordsworth kept on the right side of the account by his great faith in the goodness of man. Hazlitt thought the only way to preserve a love of mankind was to expect nothing from them, but Wordsworth was made differently. His love for man was no cold philanthropy. In the only way that can bring happiness to both subject and object, it was based on love of individual men:

> For I already had been taught to love
> My Fellow-beings;

and this chiefly in the person of the shepherd of the Cumberland hills—"A Freeman, wedded to his life of hope And hazard", "A Power or Genius, under Nature, under God, Presiding". If this individual love had for foundation no great frequency or closeness of personal contact, that only shows that Wordsworth was aware of his own limitations. If *bonhomie* is not among your endowments it is useless to pretend that it is. But his verse lights up in passion, none the less, as he speaks of his "ain folk" gathered for a Grasmere festival:

> Immense
> Is the Recess, the circumambient World
> Magnificent, by which they are embraced . . .
> How little they, they and their doings seem,
> Their herds and flocks about them, they themselves,
> And all that they can further or obstruct!
> Through utter weakness pitiably dear
> As tender infants are: and yet how great!
> For all things serve them; them the morning light
> Loves as its glistens on the silent rocks,
> And them the silent rocks which now from high
> Look down upon them. . . .

It was because his love of mankind was built upon a knowledge of the virtues of individual men—

> in the People was my trust,
> And in the virtues which mine eyes had seen—

that his faith in mankind was unshaken by the excesses of the Terror, unspeakably dreadful as these seemed to him. He saw the cause in evil leadership acting on an age-old "reservoir of guilt and ignorance". And when the fall of Robespierre brought the slaughter to an end, he saw eternal justice made manifest, and began again exultantly to scheme how "the mighty renovation" should be carried on, and earth "march firmly towards righteousness and peace". He eagerly wished that man should come out of the grub-stage,

> And spread abroad the wings of liberty,
> Lord of himself, in undisturbed delight.

And it was in a revision made in 1839 or later that he added that he would never cease to feel this aspiration. Légouis calls Wordsworth's happiness "optimism". Wordsworth was far from being an optimist in the ordinary sense of expecting the best to happen, but in the very important sense of thinking highly of mankind he was certainly a great optimist. He knew that it is right to judge human kind by its best specimens, just as it is right to judge a man by what he is at his best. And so he saw the world as a "vast abiding-place of human creatures",

> Profusely sown with individual sights
> Of courage and integrity and truth
> And tenderness.

It is almost a talisman for happiness.

I must spend a word on those who believe that love of mankind is involved not so much with happiness as with suffering on the one hand and duty on the other. Suffering can teach love, but happiness teaches no less well. What is formative in life is not kind but depth of experience. Wordsworth's experience of suffering, before 1812, was short, and though it went deep into his soul it could not undo or strongly modify the effects of the much longer experience of even deeper happiness which had been his. Wordsworth himself lent plausible support to the other view by his proposition,

> Suffering is permanent, obscure and dark,
> And has the nature of infinity.

It should be noticed that this is stated by way of antithesis to the transitoriness of *action*: had the comparison been with happiness or joy I see no reason to suppose that Wordsworth would not have allowed happiness to be illuminating where suffering is obscure and dark, to be no less permanent, and to possess equally the nature of infinity. There was a time, in 1805, when he thought that suffering had turned his way of life back upon itself; when, for a few months, he gave up his faith in joy and was driven to declare (in *Peel Castle*) that "a great distress had humanised his soul". But the poet of *Lyrical Ballads*, of *Hartleap Well*, of *Michael*, of the *Toussaint* sonnet, did not require that his soul should be humanised. *Peel Castle*, like the *Ode to Duty*, was written under the immediate stress of the death of John Wordsworth. It was only when the years had brought "tranquillity" again (for a time) that the *White Doe of*

Rylstone could be written to show beauty, love and happiness humanising a soul embittered by too deep distress. Capacity for suffering and sympathy with suffering—these are another matter, and a vital element in happiness: they may arise from suffering itself, but equally well from happiness deeply experienced. Wordsworth describes himself in the *Prelude* as "a happy man, and therefore bold to look on painful things". If it be objected that to look on painful things is not necessarily to sympathise, we may turn to *The Excursion*, and the description of the Wanderer:

> in himself
> Happy, and quiet in his cheerfulness,
> He had no painful pressure from within
> That made him turn aside from wretchedness
> With coward fears. He could *afford* to suffer
> With those that he saw suffer.

This is one of the truths about happiness that could only have been known by a man well-versed in happiness.

The *Ode to Duty* has always been a godsend to the moralists, who are rather pleased to find Wordsworth's gospel of joy apparently breaking down under the affliction of loss by death. The collapse, however, was neither permanent nor complete. Bradley quotes one of Wordsworth's friends who said, "He wrote the *Ode to Duty*, and then he had done with that matter". This, too, is not the whole truth, but certainly in his great period the path of duty was the way of joy. He did not lose sight of the "way" even in the *Ode*. The bulk of the poem is an expression of his personal need for the supporting hand of an external morality; but in the second and third stanzas he admits (doubtless with Dorothy in mind) that there is a way of life other and higher than this.

> There are who ask not if thine eye
> Be on them . . .
> Glad hearts without reproach or blot
> Who do thy work and know it not.

SOME STUDIES OF THE WAY

These are those who follow the divine law of happiness through love, unaware of duty's call yet never straying from the path.

> Serene will be our days and bright
> And happy will our natures be
> When love is an unerring light
> And joy its own security.

There, clearly stated, is the undying ideal:[1] the rest of the poem is Wordsworth's confession that he is, at the moment, finding it impossible to live up to.

The *Prelude* itself affects to end on a didactic note: Wordsworth and Coleridge are to be "blessed with true happiness" only if they can be "joint-labourers in a work" of national redemption. But the means are justified by the end in view, which is æsthetic not moral: the people are to be taught to love what they, the two poets, have loved, and to see how the mind of man may become

> A thousand times more beautiful than the earth
> On which he dwells.

Love and beauty are still the materials of happiness and spiritual growth.

ii. Peace

> Love had he found in huts where poor men lie;
> His daily teachers had been woods and rills;
> The silence that is in the starry sky,
> The sleep that is among the lonely hills.

Few passages from Wordsworth of comparable length contain so much of the essential poet. Not least to be remarked is the power of form, seen specially in the magic rhythm of the last two lines, with the protracted pause after the word "silence",

---

[1] A later exemplar of this "divine law", this "undying ideal", is to be found in Laura Ripley, "Our Grandmother", the presiding spirit of Percy Lubbock's *Earlham*.

the swift movement of the next six words, and the contrasted regularity of the pace of the fourth line. Of the many Wordsworthian ideas carried into our minds on the wave of this rhythm I wish here only to note the association of love and peace, factors of happiness which we have already seen brought together by Wordsworth in describing Margaret of the Ruined Cottage and by Dorothy in describing the lost brother.

The lines just quoted from the *Feast at Brougham Castle* present a state of inner and outward peace not easily attainable under conditions other than those so beautifully described: a peace which affords a possibility of happiness exhibiting a quality, incredible to the uninitiated but necessary if happiness is to deserve its name—the quality of continuity. Continuity of happiness, resting on an impregnable peace, may derive from various sources—from philosophy, from religion, from love. Wordsworth found it in nature.

> Through those distracting times, in nature still
> Glorying, I found a counterpoise in her
> Which, when the spirit of evil was at its height,
> Maintained for me a secret happiness.

It was the peace of long communion with nature that had, he says, removed him "from little enmities and low desires". It was on Esthwaite's shores that, in a Cambridge vacation, he found "a more than pastoral quiet in the heart of amplest projects". And he hints at the same source of peace in that lovely phrase from *The Excursion*, "the silent look of happy things", amplified in the *Prelude* to

> those unassuming things that hold
> A silent station in this beauteous world.

Shelley looked inward for peace: "The peace which sleeps within the core of the heart's heart"—or "me, within whose mind sits peace supreme". A measure of decline is to be seen in the fact that Tennyson, Browning, Arnold all expected peace only in death, "where beyond these voices there is peace". Of late there has been, perhaps, a recovery in some quarters to the high conception so admirably expressed by A. N. Whitehead: "Peace is a quality of mind steady in its assurance that fine action is treasured in the nature of things".

Wordsworth made his Solitary sigh

> For independent happiness, craving peace,
> The central feeling of all happiness.

For "central" I should myself put *basic*: peace is the basic condition on which love—the love of man or the love of woman, the love of God, the love of life—can build the edifice of happiness. Yet it is central too, when phrased in the *Prelude* as "a happy stillness of the mind"—that "stillness of soul" vainly sought by Lewis Alison in *The Fountain*. It belongs properly to happiness accumulated through long years of experience, but Wordsworth knew it early as a "calm delight" which seemed to him one of "those first-born affinities" which attuned the soul to its new existence—"a bond of union between life and joy".

If peace is to be a constituent of happiness it must be something other than placidity: it must be active, and it must result from a harmony of forces, "a dark Invisible workmanship that reconciles Discordant elements". And Wordsworth goes on, in a passage already quoted, to show how a variety of "discordant elements" in his own life have worked together to make up a "calm existence". The activity of peace consists, paradoxically, in a "wise passiveness", a noted and notable characteristic of the Wordsworthian way.

> Think you mid all this mighty sun
> Of things for ever speaking
> That nothing of itself will come,
> But we must still be seeking?

No, the poet answers his own question, we can feed our minds in a wise passiveness, and the intense receptivity of that state of mind makes the passivity constructive. More truth of a higher order, as more happiness, comes to receptive peace than from the strenuous "seekings" of the scientist. The intuitional findings of the poet-philosopher are less at the mercy of the next comer.

It is the active quality of happy peace that gives its possessor strength. Charles Morgan, a specialist in peace though not in happiness, speaks of "that exercise of the imagination which enables a man to live within his own citadel of values while material values perish". So at Cambridge, withdrawn from his native element to a milieu only half congenial, Wordsworth found his mind "busier in itself than heretofore"; he received strength and consolation as he "turned the mind in upon itself" and watched his thoughts reaching out to the limits of thought, until he perceived

> Incumbencies more awful, visitings
> Of the Upholder of the tranquil Soul,
> Which underneath all passion lives secure
> A steadfast life.

The interesting and powerful wording of this conception bears an appearance of meaning something different from the transcendent Deity into which the 1850 version turns it; it suggests rather the universal life, a sense of oneness with which is so great a source of tranquillity. A minor example, showing how some such "citadel" may stand in the heart even of a child, is seen in Wordsworth's story of the drowned man he saw recovered from Esthwaite Lake, rising with ghastly face upright from the water:

> yet no vulgar fear,
> Young as I was, a child not nine years old,
> Possessed me; for my inner eye had seen
> Such sights before, among the shining streams
> Of Fairy land.

Wordsworth's life was not a peaceful one. Yet he must have known peace, as he knew happiness, deeply. How otherwise explain the healing peace which he, more than any other poet, brings to his readers? Many a man has found peace for a troubled soul in a long steady gaze at the starry heavens. Others have derived the same effect of ineffable calm from reading the concluding lines to the poem about the Boy of Winander:

> Pre-eminent in beauty is the vale
> Where he was born and bred: the churchyard hangs
> Upon a slope above the village school;
> And through that churchyard when my way has led
> On summer evenings, I believe that there
> A long half-hour together I have stood
> Mute—looking at the grave in which he lies.

iii. God

It has been known to happen—it probably happens every day in some part or other of the world—that a man, seeing across the floor of a reception room a beautiful woman, manœuvres an introduction ... and finds her without intellect, personality, soul. Very rightly he feels cheated. Not dissimilar must be the feelings of the man without belief in God, though in either case it is possible to take refuge in Browning's apology for his "pretty woman"—"Be its beauty its sole duty!" Someone has said that "for all good pagans happiness depends on the wonder, mystery and newness of the visible world". Those things are beyond measure precious: but they are, in themselves and by themselves, hollow and without hope, like the shell of a blown egg. There are different orders of happiness, and although happiness of a high order may be built on peace and love, the highest order of all comes only out of a living touch with God.

From his youth Wordsworth recognised a twofold relation between God and joy—the word we have seen used by the two poets to express the impersonal nucleus of happiness. The sheer sense of God's immanence brought joy to him, and beyond this, the immanent God was seen as deified joy. As early as those days of "boyish sport" he saw

> The surface of the universal earth
> With triumph and delight and hope and fear
> Work like a sea;

and by his seventeenth year he "in all things saw one life, and felt that it was joy". Looking back on the same period of his life in a later book of the *Prelude* he describes his vision with greater amplitude:

> The pulse of Being everywhere was felt,
> And all the several frames of things, like stars
> Through every magnitude distinguishable,
> Were half confounded in each other's blaze,
> One galaxy of life and joy.

Not here only is Wordsworth perceived to be in sympathy with Eastern ways of thought. The Upanishads show all things created and sustained by an infinite joy. This conception continued to hold his imagination for some years. In the fourth Book of *The Excursion* (in lines dating from Racedown days) the Wanderer asserts that man, communing with the forms of nature with an understanding heart, "needs must feel the joy of a pure principle of love". After the coming of Coleridge,

> the deep enthusiastic joy,
> The rapture of the Hallelujah sent
> From all that breathes and is,

was balanced but not lessened by a new awareness of the world of man. In a passage, written in 1804, of the last Book of the *Prelude* the poet speaks (indirectly) of himself as being

> exalted by an underpresence,
> A sense of God.

A few years before this the *Tintern Abbey* lines had spoken of his sublime sense of joy at his realisation of a spirit deeply interfused through all nature and all life. And lest it should be supposed that the reference is but to a quasi-materialistic pantheism, he deliberately restates this famous passage a dozen years later, at the beginning of the last Book of *The Excursion*, and puts it (doubled in length and poetically ruined) into the mouth of the Wanderer, whose faith is elsewhere shown to be, if not narrowly orthodox, at least unmistakably Theistic. It is noticeable that the picture does not now (in the *Excursion* lines) include, nor call up, anything that can be called joyous. But it was the ideas and inspiration of the early years that provided, while they lasted, the urge and momentum for subsequent production, and constitute Wordsworth's chief claim on our æsthetic and philosophic attention.

The Creative Spirit which is constantly in the mind of the writer of the *Prelude* avoids the snares of anthropomorphism and has few attributes—life, immanence, joy, love; even when we add the Wanderer's plain Christianity, the fervent Anglicanism of the Pastor, and the careful modifications of the later *Prelude*, we still have nothing that could be closely identified with the God of revealed religion. There are indeed passages of the original *Prelude* which breathe the spirit if not the letter of orthodoxy; but the picture as a whole is of a religious sense arising from the action of imagination on reality—the only religious faculty that can play a part in creative happiness. (Witness A. N. Whitehead's praise of the Greek search for God, and "faith in a lucidity within the depth of things, to be captured by some happy glance of speculation".) Accordingly, those whose religious beliefs had come to them less directly were unable to approve. I find it half-tragic half-amusing that Wordsworth's contemporaries were so angrily alive to his discrepancies with religious orthodoxy and gave him so little credit for the profoundly religious nature of his whole vision of truth. Coleridge, kindliest if most penetrating critic of the poetry, was bitterly hostile towards the philosophy, speaking of the "vague, misty, rather than mystic, confusion of God with the world, and the accompanying nature-worship—the taint in Wordsworth's work that I most dislike as unhealthful and denounce as contagious". Even the faithful Crabb Robinson complained that Wordsworth's religion was "a sentimental and metaphysical thing in which the language of Christianity is used". Nor has his position found much more favour since his death, with respect to either the passionate earth-credo of the 1805 *Prelude*, the fervent yet serene faith of *The Excursion*, or even the curate's orthodoxy of the *Ecclesiastical Sonnets*. Wordsworth's independence of thought has always worried the bigots—much more, for instance, than the bitterer heresies of Byron and Shelley: I suppose because Wordsworth did set up as a moral and religious teacher, and did end up as a pillar of the Church. An article in Blackwood's some years ago repeated earlier censures of *The Excursion* as anti-Christian, and completed the indictment by remarking the total absence of mention of religious establishments in the *Lyrical Ballads*! A Roman Catholic writer recently complained that even in his latest stage Wordsworth was merely "Church" and not "Christian"—certainly not "Catholic" (one hears an emphatic "No, indeed!" from Grasmere churchyard). And Mr. I. A. Richards has described the "state of deep anxiety over the condition of Wordsworth's mind and fretful doubt as to the precision of his relation to the personal God of Christianity" which was caused in the breast of "a modern theological critic" by that passage in *The Excursion* where the Wanderer is described as being

> Rapt into still communion that transcends
> The imperfect offices of prayer and praise.

One sees the difficulty: the poet found God by means other than those ordained by the Book of Common Prayer, so he is little better than a heathen. It avails him nothing that Sara Coleridge once saw him stand "with one leg on the stair, declaring with an emphasis which seemed to proceed from the profoundest recesses of his soul, 'I would lay down my LIFE for the Church!'"

I am not concerned here with a precise analysis or defence of Wordsworth's religious beliefs. I desire only to show that among the constituents of his happiness was that most important one of all, religious faith arising out of a vital sense of God. And this in his creative period. Afterwards, driven by piteous need to emphasise the transcendent and personal aspect, he allowed his beliefs to fall roughly into line with the particularised creed of the Church of England, a change which prompted many of the revisions made for the published version of the *Prelude*. *The Excursion* (especially in the later books) represents a move in that direction, but from 1798 to 1811 Wordsworth believed what his own experience had shown him to be intuitively true: like the Wanderer he felt and saw God among the mountains. And the knowledge of God thus obtained gave him great joy. In the later stages joy became suspect, and the vision both of God and man lost something of its brightness. Where the original *Prelude* presents the creation as "one galaxy of life and joy", with man "of all visible natures crown", the revised text omits "joy" and substitutes the theological term "glory", at the same time reminding man that he is "born of dust and kindred to the worm"—an uncalled for glimpse of the irrelevant.

The knowledge of God can come in one of three forms of revelation, moral, mystical, or intellectual. Most people find God through a moral need, which is supplied by the Scriptures or the teaching of one of the Churches. The mystic revelation is wholly personal and incommunicable. Wordsworth's approach, though partaking of the mystical, was in the main intellectual—or æsthetic, which blends intellectual and mystical. The intellectual or æsthetic discovery of God proceeds in two stages: first the perception of the unreality of the apparently "real" or actual, and then the realisation that behind this unreal actuality is an infinite spiritual reality.[1] Wordsworth developed, at an early age a sense of the strange, elusive, unreal character of the phenomenal world. As a mere child he felt that the vanishing line of a public highway leading away from his home

> Was like an invitation into space
> Boundless, or guide into infinity.

A schoolboy, he heard at night among the solitary hills low breathings and sounds of undistinguishable motion; as he hung

[1] Perhaps it requires a third stage to identify this immanent spiritual reality with the God of whose transcendental and personal existence we may, through a different, completely mystical process, presently become aware. There is no clear evidence that Wordsworth's mystical sense ever led him to a realisation of personality in God. Such passages as that about his soul standing "naked, as in the presence of her God" sound like relics of early teaching.

on the crags seeking the raven's nest the loud wind blew through his ears with strange utterance, the sky seemed not a sky of earth, "and with what motion moved the clouds!" When the mountain seemed to stride after him in his boat on Ullswater, afterwards his brain

> Worked with a dim and undetermined sense
> Of unknown modes of being.

In London the passing crowd became

> A second-sight procession, such as glides
> Over still mountains, or appears in dreams;

and the blind beggar seemed to admonish him from another world. Often these visions were accompanied or associated with happiness. Amid the giddy bliss, he says, of childhood,

> even then I felt
> Gleams like the flashings of a shield;

and as he listened with intense delight for the answering hoot of the owls, an unexpected silence brought to his heart "a gentle shock of mild surprise" in which "the visible scene"

> Would enter unawares into his mind
> With all its solemn imagery.

He stands alone at night beneath the quiet heavens, listening to "the ghostly language of the ancient earth", and derives thence "sublimer joy" and "fleeting moods of shadowy exultation" which in after-memories filled his soul with "an obscure sense of possible sublimity". Esthwaite vale at dawn

> Appeared like something in myself, a dream,
> A prospect in my mind,

and left "a holy calm". All this experience might well take the place of the technical training demanded by Christian and other religious mystics.

Some of the experience was purely sensory, and it was Wordsworth's habit to use sense impressions (like those of the earth-sounds above) as a means to mystic knowledge. As he drank in "a pure organic pleasure" from a scene of mist and water and cloud, he "held unconscious intercourse With the eternal Beauty"—a phrase which surely means something more than the 1850 substitution, "beauty old as creation". As he rode home from boyhood excursions to Furness he felt the presence of a "still Spirit of the evening air". When he confesses to a kind of sun-worship, it is because he "had seen him lay His beauty on the morning hills". At a later time, as he walks away from Bristol, the touch of the breeze on his cheek, the simple breathing of the sweet air, are enough to bring "Trances of thought and mountings of the mind" fast upon him. Many of the "spots of time" from which his imagination drew sustenance were made up of impressions mainly of sense—a sunrise or a spectacle of clouds in moonlight, the sight of a shepherd in the fog or of a horse on the skyline. Yet ultimately sense must bow to spirit.[1] We see most clearly "into the life of things" when, blood and breath almost suspended, "we are laid asleep In body and become a living soul". The song of joy sung by all creation was to Wordsworth

> Most audible then when the fleshly ear . . .
> Forgot its function.

When the Wanderer, as a youth, beheld sunrise from the heights,

> his spirit drank
> The spectacle; sensation, soul, and form
> All melted into him; they swallowed up
> His animal being:

sensation and thought vanished before the spiritual happiness of being in the presence of God. And the last book of the *Prelude* (where so much of Wordsworth's thought finds its definitive statement) describes the highest type of mind as being

---

[1] Herford quotes the lines in which Wordsworth says the vivifying spots of time were experiences in which sense was servant, the mind "lord and master". (*Wordsworth*, p. 5.)

> By sensible impressions not enthralled,
> But by their quickening impulse made more apt
> To hold communion with the spiritual world.

The creative quality of this approach to nature can be gauged by taking a passage from the *Prelude* to which reference has already been made—

> for I would walk alone
> Under the quiet stars, and at that time
> Have felt whate'er there is of power in sound
> To breathe an elevated mood, by form
> Or image unprofaned; and I would stand,
> If the night blackened with a coming storm,
> Beneath some rock, listening to notes that are
> The ghostly language of the ancient earth,
> Or make their dim abode in distant winds:

and contrasting with it the famous passage from *Far from the Madding Crowd* containing Hardy's description of night on Egdon Heath. Hardy too has stood beneath the quiet stars, has listened to the sounds of earth and air, and describes the wind-voices with a subtlety of observation beyond Wordsworth's capacity. But how different are the results of the experience upon the two observers. Wordsworth goes on—

> Thence did I drink the visionary power;
> And deem not profitless those fleeting moods
> Of shadowy exultation: . . .
> . . . that the soul,
> Remembering how she felt, but what she felt
> Remembering not, retains an obscure sense
> Of possible sublimity, whereto
> With growing faculties she doth aspire,
> With faculties still growing, feeling still
> That whatsoever point they gain they yet
> Have something to pursue.

Hardy's only comment is that "after such a nocturnal reconnoitre it is hard to get back to earth, and to believe that the consciousness of such majestic speeding [the earth's progress through the stars] is derived from a tiny human frame" (though before the revision of 1902 he was willing to concede that by such contemplation of nature "some men may feel raised to a capability for eternity at once").

The second stage in the process went on parallel with the first. Throughout it was in a "spirit of religious love" that he walked with nature. Quite early, "with bliss ineffable",

> I felt the sentiment of Being spread
> O'er all that moves and all that seemeth still ...
> O'er all that leaps and runs and shouts and sings
> And beats the gladsome air.

In short, " in all things now I saw one life, and felt that it was joy". And now this joyous life is seen as God, at least as Godhead. The "pulse of Being" which animates the "galaxy of life and joy" reaches, among "visible natures", its crown in man because he is, "more than anything we know, instinct with Godhead". And contemplation of man brought together in great numbers for "union and communion" brings to the soul her highest joy,

> for there,
> There chiefly, hath she feeling whence she is,
> And passing through all nature rests with God.

So that at last, "out of the feeling of life endless" arises

> the great thought
> By which we live, Infinity and God.

And again in that great concluding Book of the *Prelude*, by means of a description of a sublime night-landscape, followed by an elaborate analysis of the imaginative faculty, he sets out his conception of supreme happiness. The marvellous revelation of nature which has just been given to him seemed, he says, to be the perfect image of a human mind, but one of the highest order, feeding on infinity, possessing a philosophic grasp of dominating quality, and "exalted by an underpresence, The sense of God". Such lofty minds, he says, "hold communion with the invisible world", and are "from the Deity"; and consciousness of this gives them "the highest bliss that can be known".

The ultimate deduction from these beliefs is made, more definitely than anywhere in the *Prelude*, in a fragment of verse unearthed by de Selincourt, in which Wordsworth speaks of "the one interior life"

> In which all beings live with God, themselves
> Are God.

This conception (more prominent in the literature and thought of the present day) helped Wordsworth to achieve a certain "state of being", one from which his highest poetry was born. De Selincourt provides (in a note to his edition of the *Prelude*) a brilliant analysis of this state of being. "This state, which he knew in his own experience, he often tries to describe, but it baffles description. Its essential features are (1) the overwhelming consciousness of God (2) the sense that God in Nature is one with God in the soul, so that the soul seems to *be* God or *be* Nature (3)—a natural consequence of (2)—the sense of creative power in the soul." A spiritual condition that can be thus described could not fail to fill its possessor with an exalted joy, of the kind that underlies complete happiness. Moreover, the perception of God in the universe and in the soul was attained by that intuitional process which, in the absence of mystical training, is perhaps open only to a mind made aware by happiness.

In the great "fragment" of *The Recluse*, written while the *Prelude* was still young, and afterwards placed as a "prospectus" to *The Excursion*, Wordsworth gathers up all his powers, and states—or rather touches, with the lightness that indicates complete mastery—the major headings of the Wordsworthian evangel at this time. In one perfect line, "Joy in widest commonalty spread", he suggests the idea behind my own title, and presently goes on to develop the thought, declaring that constructions of ideal happiness need not belong only to the past or to fiction:

> For the discerning intellect of Man,
> When wedded to this goodly universe
> In love and holy passion, shall find these
> A simple produce of the common day:

the human spirit, stabbed into awareness, and attuned to love and God, finds happiness in life, and in happiness life more abundantly. With the utmost clarity and emphasis he announces this "great consummation" as his "high argument", with sorrow as a not infrequent but quite secondary accompaniment, impotent to shake the central promise. In the marvellous passage which offended the Churchmen and must have frightened the later Wordsworth—where he sees himself ascending into "worlds to which the heaven of heavens is but a veil", passing unalarmed "Jehovah with his thunder", and discovering unparalleled fear and awe in "the Mind of Man, My haunt, and the main region of my song"—he anticipates the conclusions of the new cosmology; when he proclaims

> How exquisitely the individual Mind
> (And the progressive powers perhaps no less
> Of the whole species) to the external World
> Is fitted:—and how exquisitely too
> The external World is fitted to the Mind—

he is prefiguring that interaction of mind and matter which the modern scientist sees as the source of life; when he invokes the

> prophetic spirit that inspires
> The human Soul of universal earth
> Dreaming on things to come, and does possess
> A metropolitan temple in the hearts
> Of mighty poets—

he is putting before us in a sublime image both the immanence and the transcendental nature of God.

But the characteristic of the "God" of the *Prelude* and of Book I of *The Recluse* is immanence. For transcendence fully recognised we have to wait for *The Excursion*. And as transcen-

THE WAY OF HAPPINESS

dence comes in, joy goes out. This is chiefly a matter of coincidence in time, but there is also an operation of cause and effect. It is not only that the sense of an immanent God is joyous in itself, while the thought that the affairs of the world are administered by Deity gives pleasure only to a certain type of mind; what is more germane is that one feels that Wordsworth was driven to accept the idea of an external and personal supreme power as a refuge for his troubled spirit. Before 1811 he had not accepted the idea with the whole of his being, and this is clearly shown by the method of *The Excursion*, which separates out, and represents dramatically, four elements in his mind. The Solitary is the non-religious rationalist who usurped Wordsworth's brain in the period between the return from France and the settlement at Racedown; he had long left this stage behind, and was now—say in the years 1806–11—in the position shown in the person of the Wanderer, with some qualification from the figure which plays the part of the poet himself; the Pastor stands for Wordsworth's ultimate destination—and the Pastor's doctrine is orthodox enough to make the fury of the doctrinal critics absurd. It is obviously the position of the Wanderer that calls for our attention.

The Wanderer has come to know God by the processes Wordsworth himself had been through. By the awe and love inspired by the beauty of nature he came to experience high hours of "visitation from the living God", in which thought was lost in enjoyment. He had received, but had no need of, scriptural teaching: he felt and saw that God was, and the knowledge brought a mood of perpetual exaltation. Indeed, says Wordsworth, anticipating the critics, "sometimes his religion seemed to me Self-taught, as of a dreamer in the woods". The total result was, in the Wanderer's own words, "tranquillity" and "happiness"; but one feels that these came no less from the silent look of the happy things of nature than from the ideas that formed his religious faith.

The Fourth Book opens on a new note, that of transcendence, of purpose in the will of a ruling God. This is drawn forth by the need to "correct the despondency" of the Solitary. Whatever its origin, one result is that joy sinks into the background. The religion now expounded by the Wanderer for the benefit of the Solitary is one that sees life as a sad business, requiring faith in God and an after-life as support and compensation. Earth is to be despised, all we have of happiness and joy is to be relinquished, entire submission to the law of conscience is demanded. And then, suddenly, Wordsworth in his own person is "tempted to interpose". The "I" of the poem reminds the exponent of spiritual and moral uplift that a very great happiness can be derived from "pure sensations" of love for the simplest aspects of creation. And somehow this observation brings the Sage back to "earth": for the remainder of the poem he speaks, though more eloquently, the language of the *Prelude*. The happiness of the religion he has been expounding was a depressed happiness, but now he is moved to utter the inspiring declaration, "We live by admiration, hope, and love", and admits that these can be learnt by the Shepherd lad carving a dial in the turf. Presently he is speaking, in terms with which we are familiar, of an "all-pervading Spirit", and of a faculty abiding in the soul that can kindle "the encumbrances of mortal life" to "a calm, a beautiful and silent fire". Man can attain peace in himself and union with God by applying to the ear of faith the murmuring shell of the universe. As of old, nature provides impulse and inspiration; as of old, man feels "the joy of that pure principle of love". And the conclusion of the matter is that by "deeply drinking in the soul of things" we are to "build up the Being that we are": the joyous principle which had underlain the "growth of the poet's mind".

Religion is highest truth, and for Wordsworth the instrument of highest truth was the imagination, which he defined in more than one way, most briefly as "feeling intellect"—intellect guided and inspired by sympathy and love. Imagination, in this sense, has two principal ends: to make it possible to love mankind in spite of their shortcomings; and to achieve contact with, knowledge of, reality. A collateral result is the filling of the mind with a sense of mystery—the mystery of everyday life (exhibited in the lesser poems), the mystery of the beauty of nature (to which we shall return), and the mystery of the ultimate spiritual reality, to which the imagination is led by the operation of the the other two recognitions. The conscious life which Wordsworth saw in "every flower" extended to the "Soul of Nature", overflowing "with passion and with life", and thence to the infinite life of the world, to an immanent God. The subject of the *Prelude* is imagination—the mind of a poet, the mind of man; but it is equally the nature of the immanent spirit. No poet (apart from the professed religious mystics) has been so consciously and exultantly aware of the indwelling life of God. Of the two passages written for the *Prelude* containing the clearest expression of transcendence, one was never included in the poem:

> the Eternal Spirit, He that hath
> His life in unimaginable things,
> And He who painteth what He is in all
> The visible imagery of all the world....

The other, in the tenth Book, comes even nearer to Theism:

> Great God
> Who send'st thyself into this breathing world
> Through nature and through every kind of life,
> And mak'st man what he is, creature divine.

Such passages stand out a little from the general tone and intention of 1799–1805. The religious concept which served Wordsworth when he was happiest and at the height of his powers is seen rather here:

> Our destiny, our nature and our home
> Is with infinitude, and only there;

or in the famous lines,

> Wisdom and Spirit of the Universe!
> Thou Soul that art the eternity of thought!
> That giv'st to forms and images a breath
> And everlasting motion! not in vain

> ... didst Thou intertwine for me
> The passions that build up our human soul
> ... with high objects, with enduring things,
> With life and nature. ...

most plainly, perhaps, in the "presence ... a motion and a spirit" of the *Tintern Abbey* lines. Call it pantheism if you will: it is obviously not materialism, and a constant sense of participation in an infinite spiritual life bred in Wordsworth a constant joy.[1]

In the second book of *The Excursion* there is a description of the valley in which Blea Tarn lies. The poet looks down upon the "sweet recess" from the crags of Lingmoor, and expresses great delight in its beauty, seclusion and security. We are reminded of the description, in *The Recluse*, of the vale of Grasmere as seen from one of the overlooking mountains. But if we turn up this earlier word-picture we shall find in it a warmth, a passion, an exultant love and joy that are missing from the other. There seems to me a similar difference between the acquired satisfaction of the religious position which was coming to be accepted by Wordsworth and the heartfelt joy of the one that was native to his genius, and which it is evident that by 1811 he had by no means completely abandoned. It was still capable of inspiring the passage, some fifty lines in length, which has a reasonable claim to be regarded as the noblest in all *The Excursion*—that beginning with the "curious child applying to his ear the convolutions of a smooth-lipped shell", and concluding with the marvellous sound-impression of "the solitary raven flying Athwart the concave of the dark blue dome".

---

[1] Mr. S. G. Dunn convincingly demonstrates the probability that Wordsworth, seeking a metaphysical basis for his sense of the universality of being, found it in Newton's "ethereal" and highly Deistic theory of the nature of motion. ("A Note on Wordsworth's Metaphysical System", *Essays and Studies*, Vol. XVIII, 1932.)

iv. Physical Happiness

The degree of importance attached to physical sensation fluctuates with the centuries. Just now the poets are in agreement with Wordsworth and the Elizabethans. What is precious, says Stephen Spender—

> What is precious is never to forget
> The essential delight of the blood drawn from agelong springs
> Breaking through rocks in worlds before our earth.

In the school of D. H. Lawrence and the diseased brains of the Nazis this truth is exaggerated into a doctrine of "thinking with the blood", which means the surrender of reason and self-control, indeed of all the gains of a million years of evolution. In the healthier form the conception implies that we can thankfully accept our animal origin and recognise the powerful contribution that physical sensation, under control of mind, is able to make towards spiritual development. We are incompletely equipped for life unless we retain something of the alert sense and instinctive satisfactions of the lower creation. When Wordsworth heard the skylark warbling and saw the hare running races in her mirth he commented, "Even such a happy child of earth am I". Moreover, of physical sensations it is the pleasant ones that are of positive value: pain, like grief, dulls the sensibilities. "Pain", says Rabindranath Tagore, "is not an end in itself, as joy is", and Rosamund Langbridge[1] declares that "Life should be for people what it is for birds and flowers, one extended act of happiness".

This line of guidance along the way is well worth following. It acquires added significance and interest from the fact that Wordsworth was aware of it himself, as he was of his happiness as a whole. The simplest physical reaction meant much to him. "At this hour", he writes perhaps fifteen years after the experience recalled,

[1] *Charlotte Brontë: a Psychological Study* (Heinemann, 1929).

SOME STUDIES OF THE WAY

> The heart is almost mine with which I felt
> From some hill-top on sunny afternoons
> The kite high up among the fleecy clouds
> Pull at its rein.

The pleasure he is here remembering goes, of course, beyond the physical: not only do the spiritual "values" of hill-top and sunshine enter into the picture, but even the muscular response to the rhythmical pull of the kite-string contains an element of power and achievement. One perceives the same rich combination in the strain of the helm under the yachtsman's hand, and in the good heel-and-toe of the walker. Wordsworth's prowess in walking is well known, and de Quincey, in waggish but not undiscerning mood, declared that to his pedestrian habits "Wordsworth was indebted for a life of unclouded happiness, and we for much of what is best in his poetry". Certainly both by his life and in his poetry he put walking into its rightful place as the most unqualified of physical delights ("purer" than gardening, since gardening has a slender motive of gain) and the natural activity of the happy man (Leslie Stephen said of the good and wise, and one may hope that is true also). Whitman began his great *Song*,

> Afoot and lighthearted I take to the open road;
> Healthy, free, the world before me,
> The long brown path before me, leading wherever I choose.

There is cunning born of knowledge in the way in which he varies the idea in the second and third lines: "the world before me" is an abstraction; what gives joy to the heart of the walker is the instant reality of "the long brown path before me leading wherever I choose". And many writers, before and since, have done their best to remove from the word pedestrian the false connotation of "low and dull" which it bears in literary criticism. But for the sheer poetry of walking we turn to the fourth book of *The Excursion* for a passage nearly as good as the *Prelude* lines on skating. After the Wanderer has recommended the Solitary to cure his melancholy by rising with the lark and

87

climbing the crags of Lingmoor, Wordsworth in his own person breaks into dithyramb:

> Oh what a joy it were, in vigorous health,
> To have a body (this our vital form
> With shrinking sensibility endued
> And all the nice regards of flesh and blood)
> And to the elements surrender it
> As if it were a spirit!—How divine
> The liberty for frail, for mortal, man
> To roam at large among unpeopled glens
> And mountainous retirements, only trod
> By devious footsteps; regions consecrate
> To oldest time; and, reckless of the storm
> That keeps the raven quiet on her nest
>   ... to roam
> An equal among mightiest energies. ...

Only a poet walks like that, but the ordinary walker knows something of the poet's joy and divine liberty, with consequent profit in happiness to the whole of life.

The passage calls to mind that other splendid expression of physical happiness, the lines from *Saul* beginning,

> Oh the wild joy of living! the leaping from rock up to rock,
> The strong rending of boughs from the firtree, the cool silver shock
> Of the plunge in a pool's living water. ...

Browning's lines provide a contrast to Wordsworth's, not only in their strong oriental colouring but in their concern merely with the "coarser pleasures" and "animal movements" which Wordsworth associated with his "boyish days", but the conclusion is sound, hyperbole remaining only in the word "ever"—

> How good is man's life, the mere living! how fit to employ
> All the heart and the soul and the senses for ever in joy!

For the quieter but no less intense joy of real outdoor life—

outdoor life in England—we turn again to Wordsworth, and the opening of the *Prelude*, with the gentle breeze which beats against the truant poet's cheek, a messenger bringing joy. There is much here, again, that is not of the body—the pleasures of thought and hope, of love and poetry; but the basic feeling is pure happiness of sensation and physical health. The same relation, but inverted, is seen in that part of the *Tintern Abbey* poem where Wordsworth remembers how in his early twenties

> like a roe
> I bounded o'er the mountains, by the sides
> Of the deep rivers and the lonely streams:

this is the physical rapture, but it springs now from a spiritual emotion indicated in the next lines:

> more like a man
> Flying from something that he dreads than one
> Who sought the thing he loved. For nature then
> To me was all in all.

The nature-passion is of the soul, but like the passion of human love, it electrifies the body.

There is no alienation of mind from body in Wordsworth. "Sensations sweet, felt in the blood and felt along the heart", presently pass into the "purer mind". There is a subtle confusion of states in the diagnosis of "many a thoughtless hour"—

> when, from excess
> Of happiness, my blood appeared to flow
> With its own pleasure, and I breathed with joy—

blood and breath have conscious sensations of their own. The unusual quality of Wordsworth's happiness was in part due to the fact that it was a nice blend of sense impressions and imaginative exaltation, the inferior, primitive ingredients giving "body" to the mixture. A beautiful illustration of the way in which the two states were combined, or even identified, in his happiness, occurs in the original version of the *Prelude* just before the meeting with the lank and ghastly soldier.

> Thus did I steal along that silent road,
> My body from the stillness drinking in
> A restoration like the calm of sleep,
> But sweeter far. Above, before, behind,
> Around me, all was peace and solitude.
> I looked not round, nor did the solitude
> Speak to my eye; but it was heard and felt.
> Oh, happy state! what beauteous pictures now
> Rose in harmonious imagery—they rose
> As from some distant regions of my soul,
> And came along like dreams, yet such as left
> Obscurely mingled with their passing forms
> A consciousness of animal delight,
> A self-possession felt in every pause
> And every gentle movement of my frame.

In another place, showing how one state can slide imperceptibly into the other, he speaks of certain moments

> when the light of sense
> Goes out, but with a flash that has revealed
> The invisible world.

This is almost the mystical function, but the "revelation" would seem to be intellectual or æsthetic, not religious. Yet we have seen how the joy that Wordsworth drew from pure sense-impressions was of great importance to his mystic approach to God. The intimate connection between sense, intellect and happiness is recognised again when he describes

> Those hallowed and pure motions of the sense
> Which seem, in their simplicity, to own
> An intellectual charm . . . and constitute
> The bond of union between life and joy.

It is an instance of the originality of Wordsworth's outlook that he should see simplicity rather than complexity as a mark of intellectual quality; but the vital truth conveyed by the lines is that the gulf between physical life and the spiritual state of joy is not easily bridged for the understanding, and that a practicable link is found in the kind of sensation that he is picturing.

Emphatically, it is through the senses that the education of the mind by nature is affected. The poet was

> well pleased to recognise
> In nature and the language of the sense
> The anchor of my purest thoughts, the nurse,
> The guide, the guardian of my heart, and soul
> Of all my moral being.

It is by sense-impressions that nature—"the mighty world of eye and ear"—works. To the boy blowing mimic hootings to the owls over Windermere it was the voice of mountain torrents that was carried far into his heart, and the visible scene that entered unawares into his mind. On "Lucy" the exquisite happiness of the results is shown with unparalleled beauty in the poem, *Three Years She Grew*. Nature is to be to the girl "both law and impulse", in the vital sense that must precede the moral:

> She shall be sportive as the fawn
> That wild with glee across the lawn
> Or up the mountain springs;
> And hers shall be the breathing balm,
> And hers the silence and the calm
> Of mute insensate things.

There follows presently what is perhaps the most understanding comment ever made on a woman's loveliness:

> and she shall lean her ear
> In many a secret place
> Where rivulets dance their wayward round,
> *And beauty born of murmuring sound*
> *Shall pass into her face:*

beauty, shall we say, which is one part feature, one part expression, and two parts, or half, happiness; and "born", as to its immediate occasion, from pure sense impression. I do not know where to look for equal insight unless to that lovely couplet in which the effect of spiritual happiness is perfectly observed and expressed:

> A countenance in which did meet
> Sweet records, promises as sweet.

If in a way the physical element in both Wordsworth's happiness and his poetical apparatus is the least important, it is not the least fascinating. Indeed, the more one thinks of primitive sense as a means of communication between the mind and spiritual reality the stranger and more wonderful it becomes. It is worth noting that the senses, as a vehicle of truth, have lately been coming into their own among thinkers more cautious than poets. The compilers of the classical systems of philosophy generally began by ruling out sense-perception as obviously fallacious, but Whitehead now suggests that "in the higher animal types" there is a tendency for sense-perception to conform with reality. When Wordsworth's "boyish days and their glad animal movements" were "all gone by", the mysticism which succeeded was still rooted in sense. De Quincey said Wordsworth's intellectual passions were fervent and strong but rested on a basis of preternatural sensibility diffused through all the animal passions and appetites. And apart from their strength the quality of his physical sensations (leading him to "recognise a grandeur in the beatings of the heart") was such that they were virtually indistinguishable from spiritual experiences; and this points to a possibility that body and soul are more closely associated than is commonly supposed: that they are in fact one and the same thing—the body the material aspect of the soul, the soul the spiritual reality of the body, so that the sense life of the body is part of the spiritual life of the soul.

v. Beauty

It was "beauty of the inward soul" that Socrates implored of Pan in the immortal prayer that closes the *Phaedrus*, but the flame that lures the poet, and all artists, is objective beauty. Of objective beauty there are three kinds: those discoverable in nature, in the human form, and in works of art. Of art Wordsworth seems to have had little vital appreciation: he was indifferent to music, though of course he delighted in the "passion and power" of "words in tuneful order"; he admired the paintings of Sir George Beaumont (though he showed excellent taste in the cases of the real masters); and he dismissed the triumphs of architecture in one sweeping phrase, "the mean and vulgar works of man"—and if later he made an exception in favour of King's Chapel it was apparently (as with Erasmus before the Carthusian cloister at Pavia) the thought of the cost of the building that came first into his mind. With the beauty of women Wordsworth was as little concerned as any poet who ever lived (which was just as well, since Mary had a squint and all Coleridge could say of Dorothy's appearance was that if you expected a plain woman you found her pretty and if you expected a pretty one you thought her plain)—though here again we have seen that he could appraise the elements of beauty in a girl's face with masterly tact.

To Wordsworth beauty meant nature, and if this is a limitation, he used his limits so well that they are barely noticeable. The poet who "grew up fostered alike by beauty and by fear", "holding unconscious intercourse With the eternal Beauty", and finding in the Spirit of Nature "the soul of beauty and enduring life", won a continuous joy which is one of the planes of happiness. Abstract beauty (John Masefield's muse) hardly entered his scheme. For a moment you think you have it in *The Recluse*, where he cries, "Beauty, a living presence of the earth!" but it is the pervading substantial beauty of the vale of Grasmere that he has in mind and proceeds to hymn:

> Beauty, a living presence of the earth,
> Surpassing the most fair ideal Forms
> Which craft of delicate spirits hath composed
> From earth's materials, waits upon my steps,
> Pitches her tent before me as I move,
> An hourly neighbour.

It is, too, that best of all natural beauty, the beauty of one's own country, which, in the words of the Wanderer, inspires the "active powers" of the mind to

> sweep distemper from the busy day,
> And make the chalice of the big round year
> Run o'er with gladness, whence the Being moves
> In beauty through the world, and all who see
> Bless him, rejoicing in his neighbourhood.

Here beauty and happiness, if not indistinguishable are at least indissoluble.

The tones of love and the passion of rhythmic form come into his verse when it turns to nature, for example in the first book of the *Prelude*, when, after the somewhat arid search for a historical or philosophic theme for song, he breaks lyrically out—

> Was it for this
> That one, the fairest of all Rivers, loved
> To blend his murmurs with my nurse's song?—

and continues in unspoilt loveliness for over two hundred lines. Love and beauty are inseparably mingled. Only love could see beauty with such visionary clearness, only supreme beauty could excite such love. "Love", said Plato, "is birth in beauty—conception and bringing forth in beauty.... Love leads at last to the perception of absolute beauty." Wordsworth's love for nature led him to perceive God in nature, and God is absolute beauty.

When we speak of Wordsworth's love for nature, and think of him deriving happiness and imaginative vision from intercourse with nature, it is desirable to remember that such love and intercourse meant, for him, something more than they mean for most people—something more than just living in the country. In a sublime passage of the *Prelude* he tells of his heart's "more exact and intimate companionship" with nature long loved but before imperfectly known; and of the joy of life

> When every hour brings palpable access
> Of knowledge, and all knowledge is delight.

To him the seasons "unfolded transitory qualities" which, under "the watchful power of love", "left a register of permanent relations" and "silent unobtrusive sympathies". Walking alone he "drank the visionary power" and derived "fleeting moods of shadowy exultation", which endowed his soul with "an obscure sense of possible sublimity" whereto it might endlessly aspire. It is in the light of such a confession that we are able to understand what he meant when he said he found in nature a "counterpoise" to evil which maintained for him "a secret happiness". When he is trying to tell us what nature was to him in early manhood he uses the strongest words he can find, "passion" and "appetite", and the words are to be taken in their extreme and literal sense. He says, "the sounding cataract Haunted me like a passion"—and he says it with amazement, remembering himself caught and lost in the torrent of that tremendous love. "The tall rock, The mountain and the deep and gloomy wood Were then to me an appetite", he says—and we can see him seeking them out with irresistible desire. And if these "wild ecstasies" grew more sober with the years, their formative impression on the whole being of the poet remained. Only so can the beauty of nature become an element in happiness of soul and the adored ritual of a living religion. Wordsworth walked with nature in a "spirit of religious love", and his æsthetic faith is built on the mystery of the beauty of nature.

It is, again, only in the light of this passionate intensity of feeling that we can understand the creative power to which Wordsworth more than once refers. Coleridge seems to have thought it a weakness—

> Oh William, we receive but what we give,
> And in our life alone doth nature live.

But Wordsworth accepts the fact that we both perceive and "half-create":

> An auxiliar light
> Came from my mind which on the setting sun
> Bestowed new splendour . . . and the midnight storm
> Grew darker in the presence of my eye.

And the possession of this "creative sensibility", this "plastic power", increased his obeisance, his devotion, his transport. It is not often that he lets the imaginative vision take the form of personification on any "creative" scale, but when he does so it is with convincing success—we ourselves are endowed with the new vision. In the superb passage from *The Recluse* beginning, "Bleak season was it, turbulent and bleak", he makes the face of nature look sternly on the two travellers, himself and Dorothy, "journeying side by side", "parted and reunited by the blast". The trees, the brooks, question them as they pass:

> "What would ye," said the shower,
> "Wild wanderers, whither through my dark domain?"
> The sunbeam said, "Be happy!"

Grasmere vale meets them "with a passionate welcoming", and having first proved the temper of their minds with two months of sullen storm it now "begins to love" them.

The attitude may be fallacious, as Coleridge and afterwards Ruskin objected, but only if we rank the knowledge of the botanist and the geologist above that of the poet; to ban it would be to lose the illumination of the exquisite comment on

> those unassuming things that hold
> A silent station in this beauteous world.

But Wordsworth's more characteristic way was to expose his mind to the spectacle of the beauty of nature, with all its inherent values, in a "wise passivity". He says, "I felt, and nothing else. I did not judge". If he strayed from the path, and ceased for a time to stand in nature's presence "a sensitive and a creative soul", he was restored to himself by Dorothy, of whom he wrote,

> Whate'er the scene presented to her view,
> That was the best, to that she was attuned.

So Wordsworth himself: he was wakeful to nature's daily face of beauty "even as waters are to the sky's motion". It is only such an attitude of receptive passivity, passionate acceptance, that can lead to the deepest of all effects—the entry of beauty into what is called the unconscious. Wordsworth more than once makes it plain that he is aware of this effect. He tells how in childhood

> nature by extrinsic passion first
> Peopled my mind with beauteous forms or grand;

how he derived thence "hallowed and pure motions of the sense"; how he "drank a pure organic pleasure"; so that "by pleasure and repeated happiness" and "by force of obscure feelings", the beauteous scenes depicted in his brain "were by invisible links allied to the affections". Into this class of effect we can put the result of the memorable vision of the sunrise he witnessed as he came home over Ligging Shaw during his first Cambridge vacation. Those "vows" that were then made for him, that "bond" unknown to him that was given, that he was to be "a dedicated spirit"—this suggests an operative effect on the unconscious mind by reason of which he was able to say, many years later, that the "blessedness" of the moment even yet remained.

This great dedicatory vision came to Wordsworth when he was alone. Solitude was precious, but not necessary, to him: the creative moments of the Alps he shared with Jones, as he must have shared many other such moments with Dorothy and Coleridge, and he was not physically alone when he saw the most sublime of all his spectacles of nature, the moon cloudscape of the concluding book of the *Prelude*. Yet solitude does withdraw the last veil from the face of nature, and for Wordsworth, as for his "poet", impulses of deeper birth came to him in solitude. Most of his mystic experiences, all associated with natural beauty, occurred when he was alone, and he loved a public way at night because then

> in its silence it assumes
> A character of deeper quietness
> Than pathless solitudes.

More than once Wordsworth couples beauty and fear, and

Professor Havens is inclined to stress the second element.[1] In fact he suggests that it was not the beauty of nature at all that attracted Wordsworth, since he rejoiced in such phenomena as fog and storm. It is only people with delicate nerves who fail to find beauty and grace "even in the motion of the storm", and though fog can be obscuring and depressing (as Wordsworth admits in the *Guide to the Lakes*) it has exquisite varieties, and when Wordsworth drew "a pure organic pleasure from the lines of curling mist" it was not ugliness that produced the profound effect indicated by the use of the word "organic". As for fear, it is an æsthetic not a moral emotion that is intended in such an expression as "fostered alike by beauty and by fear", or in the "huge and mighty forms" which troubled the young Wordsworth's dreams after the night adventure with the boat on Ullswater: an intense form of wonder, producing an effect of katharsis. Wordsworth counts among the "beneficent influences" of his childhood the feeling of "visionary dreariness" that came to him on wind-beaten, gibbet-haunted Penrith Beacon. In one of the admirable passages written for but never included in the *Prelude*, he speaks of lightning and its concomitants as "objects of fear, yet not without their own enjoyment". An imaginative appreciation of the beauty of nature necessarily includes a strong element of awe, but exaggeration of this element out of due proportion would have been inconsistent with Wordsworth's mental and physical soundness.

Nature is always, with Wordsworth, what Goethe called "the living mantle of God" and Wordsworth himself "the breath of God", but he seldom mixed nature up with man. The loveliest of his nature pieces are exalted into an almost unearthly beauty by being removed from all human association. Thus he has stood on the Westmorland shore at evening just before moonrise, a stranger, moved by nothing but the pure beauty of the scene before him:

---

[1] Dr. J. C. Smith too. But the only instance he gives which lies outside my generalisation—the panic in John's Grove—seems to be one of simple physical terror.

> yet I have stood,
> Even while mine eye has moved o'er three long leagues
> Of shining water, gathering, as it seemed,
> Through every hair-breadth of that field of light
> New pleasure, like a bee among the flowers.

Sometimes, however, his mood is different. One of the reasons why the fair vale of Grasmere and its spacious heights were dear to William and Dorothy was that,

> Look where we will, some human hand hath been
> Before us with its offering,

so that the whole vale "swarms with sensation". His native hills are the lovelier because

> The elements and seasons in their change
> Do find their dearest fellow labourer there,

because the district breathes on all sides "the fragrance of humanity"; and it is humanity in the guise of beauty, "Man free, man working for himself, with choice of time and place and object", and having, through his way of life, a certain "simplicity, and beauty, and inevitable grace". He establishes an interesting relation between two states of happiness, into both of which both nature and humanity enter. Best of all, he says, is

> The bliss of walking daily in life's prime
> Through field or forest with the maid we love—

to have a home with her in some deep vale; and next to this "dear delight" comes the joy of wandering on, a solitary poet, through field and grove and over naked moors, and to

> Converse with men, where, if we meet a face,
> We almost meet a friend.

Wordsworth the nature lover had no more of the misanthrope than most of us. In later years he neither felt himself, nor was felt by others to be, out of place at Lamb's or Haydon's convivial parties.

Somewhere between nature and man (perhaps nearer to nature, though not too distant from the small children of man) come the animals. Once the warm-blood stage is reached, the animal creation is almost universally beautiful, and it was one of God's greatest jokes to have selected the most marked of the exceptions to be the ancestor of man (though I think we can claim to have made the best of a bad start). Wordsworth saw endless beauty and much happiness among animals and birds, and drew very great happiness himself therefrom. Keats and Shelley read "joyance" into the songs of nightingale and lark, but were themselves plunged into despondency by contrast. A comparison of *The Cuckoo* with the bird poems of any other writer (save Meredith's *Lark Ascending*) shows Wordsworth entering into the bird's "blitheness" by means of his own personal happiness where the other poets are either melancholy or detachedly observant. The innocent children of nature move and inspire him. After a long pause in the composition of the *Prelude* he is stirred to continue by the voices of "a little Band, a Quire of Redbreasts", and when presently he sees a Glow-worm shining clear——

> silence touched me then
> No less than sound had done before; the Child
> Of Summer, lingering, shining by itself,
> The voiceless Worm on the unfrequented hills,
> Seemed sent on the same errand with the Quire
> Of Winter that had warbled at my door,
> And the whole year seemed tenderness and love.

We learn much about Wordsworth when we visualise that great poem, lying inert and stubborn as the Bowder Stone of Borrowdale, being set going by that small though exquisite prompting. At Grasmere, he enumerates the creatures that are soon to become his friends—the small grey horse that bears the paralytic man, the donkey (though he must refer to it as "the patient brute in Scripture sanctified"), blackbird and thrush and a pair of eagles, the owl of Owlet Crag, the heifer and its mother. And he tells how it was not till youth was past that

SOME STUDIES OF THE WAY

> The inferior creatures, beast or bird, attuned
> My spirit to that gentleness of love,
> Won from me those minute obeisances
> Of tenderness, which I may number now
> With my first blessings.

Thus, when the hour came for him to devote a whole great poem to his sense of the strange power of beauty, it was on an animal that his choice fell as the instrument of his allegory. I suppose beauty did not mean quite so much to Wordsworth as it did to Keats. Yet there is always the *White Doe of Rylstone*, where Wordsworth does a thing that even Keats, even Marlowe, might not have dared to do: to restore a bruised, lacerated and dying soul to health and happiness by the simple application of beauty in so ingenuous a form that it could be figured as an animal. One of the vital truths of *The White Doe* is that if beauty is to form part of the fabric of happiness it must be brought to life by love. Harper enters fully into the greatness of the poem, and calls it "the final message of Wordsworth's personal religion". He learns from it that "only Nature, Mind and the Peace of God endure". But he overlooks the beautiful picture with which the story closes, of the "consecrated maid" happy at last through love. In her case it was not love of God. So far as the story goes, her salvation came through simple love for the beautiful creature which gives the poem its name: it was this innocent and unexalted love that softened Emily's heart and brought her through her sorrow to happy peace. Action, as Wordsworth said, the heroic action of the narrative, had failed: the wise passiveness of a heart released from suffering by love reached "the purest sky of undisturbed mortality".

Yet I think the authentic theme of *The White Doe* is not love but beauty. There was a good deal of controversy about the poem at the time when it was written, and I can well understand Wordsworth's impatience with Lamb and Coleridge, who wanted to "improve the structure" of the narrative part. The narrative does indeed stand in need of clarification, but the only incidents that matter, those which constitute the appalling afflictions of Emily, are clear enough. As Wordsworth insisted, "the true action of the poem is spiritual", and others among its admirers have failed adequately to enunciate its spiritual message. Raleigh, for instance, stops short in his exposition at the point where Emily has been brought

> To the subjection of a holy,
> Though stern and rigorous, melancholy,

under which she is pointedly described by the poet as "a joyless human being". But this is a consummation quite alien to Wordsworth's philosophy, and the lesson of the poem, which becomes clear only after this, is not joyless endurance under loss, but the assimilation of loss and the rebirth of happiness. What the White Doe itself stands for must remain uncertain: perhaps religion, perhaps love, but something entirely spiritual; for me the lovely creature represents the spirit of beauty. Emily's grief was harsh and ugly. Now the White Doe comes, or comes back, to bring beauty into her life, and presently we find her yielding to "a very gladness", "a deeper peace". Her soul is now blest

> With a soft spring-day of holy,
> Mild, and grateful melancholy—

and mark how deliberately the terms of this couplet are opposed to those of the one previously quoted. At last happiness itself descends upon her: the word "happy" occurs now for the first time in the poem:

> When she from the abyss returned
> Of thought, she neither shrunk nor mourned;
> Was happy that she lived to greet
> Her mute companion.

A noble spirit, led by beauty out of joyless grief to a still happiness of love: this is the theme of *The White Doe of Rylstone*.

There were moments when Wordsworth's confidence in his perception of spiritual truth wavered, but his faith in the blessing of beauty was rooted unshakably in his deepest intuitions.

> If this
> Be but a vain belief, yet oh, how oft ...
> O sylvan Wye, thou wanderer through the woods,
> How often has my spirit turned to thee!

In the *Prelude*, after a supreme exposition of his understanding of the joyous soul of the world, he says again,

> If this be error, and another faith
> Find easier access to the pious mind,

yet will he stand fast and testify to what nature, the mountains, lakes and cataracts, mists and winds, have done for him, making him, he hopes, pure in heart, content with modest pleasures, free from little enmities and low desires. The times are full of fear, but he retains a faith that fails not in all sorrow; and he ends his hymn of praise,

> The gift is thine, O Nature! Thou hast fed
> My lofty speculations; and in thee
> For this uneasy heart of ours I find
> A never-failing principle of joy
> And purest passion.

So completely, so integrally, is objective beauty united in Wordsworth with Socrates' "beauty of the inward soul".

vi. Truth

You may find in the Wordsworth letters a little story which pleasantly illustrates the two everyday varieties of truth—moral and intellectual. Dorothy is writing to Mrs. Clarkson about an old Lakeland woman who, she says, "remembers you with the greatest affection". She goes on: "I read her your last letter, adding a few words from you, which were not there, of remembrance of her and her daughter, and she was so pleased both with that remembrance and the whole letter that I resolved I would write to you ... to have some true message from your own self to her and your daughter". Isn't it characteristic of Dorothy —whose kindness of heart was matched by her fearless mind —that her one recorded lapse from the path of moral veracity should have been just this! And she shows her mental grasp of the transaction when she goes on, "I flatter myself that in the spirit, though not in the letter [was she aware of the pun?], what I made you say was just and true", and adds discerningly, "Indeed if I had not felt it to be so I should have been wounded instead of pleased by her pleasure". That is a test which only an intellectually as well as a morally honest person would have seen to be applicable.

We are not concerned here with moral truth, and only to a small extent with intellectual. Judgments arrived at by intellectual processes are important and necessary; they are also richly satisfying—to the intellect, but they are always at the mercy of an additional argument or an overlooked premise. Wordsworth did not underestimate intellect. He told Sir George Beaumont "there is no happiness except by intellect" (he added "and virtue"), but he got little happiness out of his closely argued cases against the Bishop of Llandaff and the Convention of Cintra. He found more happiness in asserting wild, illogical, indisputable truths like

> One impulse from a vernal wood
> May teach you more of man,
> Of moral evil and of good
> Than all the sages can.

The impulse, as the remainder of the poem indicates, is an impulse of exalted happiness, and the statement made in the stanza quoted appears absurd only to those who have not experienced the illumination of happiness. Joy, says Tagore, is knowledge in its completeness, it is knowing with our whole being. A more usual claim is that a miraculous perception of truth may arise out of the experience of love—"Love wakes men, once a lifetime each". Bernard Shaw makes John Tanner declare that the moment he knew himself in love with Anne he was dowered with a blindingly new and true understanding of life. We are given no proof of the supposed access of insight, which seems to have been as impermanent as the amatory condition. More convincing is Tolstoy's picture of Pierre in love with Natasha. When Pierre's feeling is at its height Tolstoy describes it as "blissful insanity", and says, "All the views he formed of men and circumstances at this time remained true for him always". He makes Pierre say of himself, "I was then wiser and had more insight than at any other time, and understood all that is worth understanding in life, because ... because I was happy". That, I think, is the point. Insight into truth depends ultimately upon happiness. Other faculties—combined under Wordsworth's term "feeling intellect"—may go deep, but happiness carries understanding through one last degree of penetration. And happiness itself springs generally, as we have seen, from a combination of states of which love is essentially one. Tanner may have been in love: he was certainly not happy.

The possession of truth is sometimes said to bring happiness. If so it must be imaginative truth of spirit: mere knowledge is admitted often to work the other way. It was truth, but imaginative truth, that Arnold meant by "light" when he wrote: "Joubert loved the light. His whole body was full of light. And because he was full of light he was also full of happiness. . . . For certainly it is natural that the love of light, which is already in some measure the possession of light, should irradiate—beatify the whole life of him who has it. There is something unnatural and shocking where, as in the case of Coleridge, it does not."

Interesting, that aside on Coleridge. Coleridge was the most intensely religious man within my knowledge, but, as Arnold says, he was not happy. And this was partly due to a certain attitude to truth. He said in 1832, "Were it possible for me even to *think* otherwise (i.e. than on orthodox lines about God), the very grass in the fields would turn black before my eyes". Truth is fixed, and he has fixed it!—if truth should prove not to accord with his preconceptions, truth and life can go together. What an attitude for a philosopher!

But in the Wordsworth gospel, <u>truth is born of happiness</u>, not happiness of truth. In the *Tintern Abbey* lines, after beauty and peace have induced a mood in which the distractions of common life are lost, harmony and joy bring understanding:

> While with an eye made quiet by the power
> Of harmony and the deep power of joy
> We see into the life of things.

And not only "see into" but can communicate—

> In common things that round us lie
> Some random truths he can impart—
> The harvest of a quiet eye
> That broods and sleeps on his own heart.

The lesser truths of morality might be learnt (at Cambridge) "through dislike and most offensive pain", but in spheres of greater permanence it was nature and love that

> led me back through opening day
> To those sweet counsels between head and heart
> Whence grew that genuine knowledge fraught with peace.

From the negative side you have the Wanderer declaring the impossibility of achieving knowledge of God "in a gloom of uninspired research"—

> Meanwhile, the heart within the heart, the seat
> Where peace and happy consciousness should dwell,
> On its own axis restlessly revolving,
> Seeks, yet can nowhere find, the light of truth.

And the *Ode* places "all that is at enmity with joy" among the chief obstacles to the perception of truths which are never to die.

With Wordsworth truth rose generally out of that other instrument of happiness, beauty, the beauty of nature. Beauty and truth are by him not identified: beauty is a means to truth. We have seen how, the more closely he pressed to nature, the more his happiness increased, but his power of understanding grew too. "Now", he says, "to nature's finer influences my mind lay open":

> Many are the joys
> Of youth; but oh! what happiness to live
> When every hour brings palpable access
> Of knowledge, when all knowledge is delight
> And sorrow is not there.

Nature and delight go hand in hand with knowledge and truth —truth of God and man. His over-emphatic scorn for "the mean and vulgar works of man" is the reflection of a sense (only partly justified) that they are further from ultimate reality than the "forms and images" of nature. So he hymns the "Wisdom and Spirit of the Universe" that has purified for him the elements of feeling and thought by intertwining his growing passions with "high objects, with enduring things, with life and nature". The education of nature helped him to see man himself more clearly. He first "looked at man through objects that were great and fair"; he had been free and happy and close to beauty, and therefore,

> starting from this point,
> I had my face towards the truth, began
> With an advantage; furnished with that kind
> Of prepossession without which the soul
> Receives no knowledge that can bring forth good,
> No genuine insight ever comes to her.

As a speculative philosopher Wordsworth was much inferior to Coleridge. Yet a great modern thinker (A. N. Whitehead) has declared that "the chief danger in philosophy is that dialectic deductions from inadequate formulæ should exclude direct intuitions from explicit attentions". It was by just such intuitions, not by reasoning—not by intellect but by "feeling intellect"—that truth came to Wordsworth. When he tells of how he was taught truth, he mentions "intellectual power from stage to stage Advancing", but associates it with "love, joy and imagination". His understanding of truth, as of happiness, was poetic and intuitional. His letters show him a man of strong common sense and sound judgment, with an occasional flash of inspiration in matters of landscape gardening. In verse, even, when he is consciously moralising he is not more often right than "my brother the Dean" would have been in his sermons. But when love and beauty and happiness join with the rhythmic urge of the poetic afflatus, then do the stars come out; then the serene heaven that vaults the Wordsworthian way is inlaid with patines of bright truth. One such celestial gleam may give us an interpretation of human life—

> Our birth is but a sleep and a forgetting;

another an obvious yet unacknowledged ethical maxim—

> Never to blend our pleasure or our pride
> With sorrow of the meanest thing that feels;

a third a much-needed reminder that "the very world which is the world of all of us" is

> the place in which, in the end,
> We find our happiness or not at all.

We shall find a key to the mystic touch upon reality in

> those obstinate questionings
> Of sense and outward things,
> Fallings from us, vanishings,
> Blank misgivings of a creature
>   Moving about in worlds not realised;

a clue to the poet's secret in—

> Come forth, and bring with you a heart
> That watches and receives.

We catch a glimpse of nature's power in the promise to Lucy—

> Myself will to my darling be
> Both law and impulse;

we are told something about woman which it is unwise ever to forget—

> a spirit still, and bright
> With something of angelic light;

we learn of the magic Meredithian sympathy that may exist between man and nature—

> Then, dearest maiden, move along these shades
> In gentleness of heart; with gentle hand
> Touch—for there is a spirit in the woods.

Glowing imagination may show life as a transparency:

> O blessed bird! the earth we pace
> Again appears to be
> An unsubstantial, faery place
> That is fit home for thee;

exquisite fancy may bring lost loveliness back to life—

> Yet some maintain that to this day
> She is a living child;
> That you may see sweet Lucy Gray
> Upon the lonesome wild.

And a slender lyric may hold in crystal distillation a whole world's agelong wisdom, heights and depths of philosophy: the assimilation of death by life, acceptance of tragic loss through love and happiness:

> A slumber did my spirit seal;
>   I had no human fears;
> She seemed a thing that could not feel
>   The touch of earthly years.
> No motion has she now, no force;
>   She neither hears nor sees;
> Rolled round in earth's diurnal course
>   With rocks, and stones, and trees.

To me it seems indisputable that happiness clears the vision, brightens the faculties, and brings truth nearer like a telescope, but the same claim is sometimes perversely made for sorrow.

Perhaps all one ought to say is that some men, Milton, Arnold, Beethoven, Dante, have drawn wisdom from the dark, while for others, among whom is certainly Wordsworth and perhaps Shakespeare, the light of joyous experience has been more revealing. When Wordsworth speaks of the sadder side of life he is not more profound than another; when happiness is his text he is almost always deeply original and true. The *Tintern Abbey* lines contain four observations, three of them doubtful or commonplace, on life considered as a burden, a fever, a dreary intercourse, against more than a score of brilliant flashes into the very heart of happiness. And in that place where Wordsworth, more than anywhere else, attempts a comprehensive account of his sense of life (in the reflections that resulted on the moonlight vision on Snowdon, in the last book of the *Prelude*) it is neither pure intellect that is described as the instrument nor pure knowledge that is achieved. Man, at his highest, he says, has at command a "glorious faculty" which from small suggestions caught from the ordinary world of life can build great imaginative constructions of "the whole compass of the universe", and which, being spiritual, can influence that universe to spiritual ends. And what comes to minds which possess and exercise this perceptive and creative faculty is not only wisdom and power but life and happiness—"the highest bliss that flesh can know", arising out of the consciousness that they are of God.

. . . . .

[The concluding sentence of this chapter is based on what I think is the true reading of the *Prelude* (1850) XIV. 115. Lines 113–116 run:

>   the highest bliss
> That flesh can know is theirs—the consciousness
> Of Whom they are, habitually infused
> Through every image and through every thought.

Professor Havens thinks that *by* is required between "Of" and "Whom", and that the comma after "are" is redundant: "the consciousness of by Whom they are habitually infused—the consciousness of being habitually infused by God". It seems more likely that Wordsworth intended the comma, and that the missing word is another *of* before "Of Whom". Their bliss arises from the consciousness of "of Whom they are", consciousness of the fact that they are of God, "from the Deity" (line 112); and this consciousness is habitually infused through every image and thought. This reading does least violence to Wordsworth's construction. If he had been in the habit of using "weak endings" he could have avoided all difficulties by writing

> the knowledge that
> They are of God. . . .]

CHAPTER V

The Necessity of Happiness

AND NOW—why all this insistence on happiness, that "sickliest of human ideals", as it has been called? Let us note in passing that the author of the remark was Mr. L. P. Jacks, who was brought up on Carlyle, and by that fact "conditioned" to despise happiness and reverence duty. By now the spell is weaker, and we are free to realise that men are at their best only when they are happy. There is more permanence in the Greek way of thinking than in the Victorian, and the conception of the end of right living prompted by a reading of Wordsworth is closer to the free-blooming excellence, the shining perfection, of the Greek ἀρετή than to the harsh ideal of duty preached by our twisted Christianity. I say "twisted" because I believe the way of life taught and followed by Jesus was not opposed to the Greek ideal. The motive force of conduct according to Jesus was not duty but love, which is a form of beauty and happiness. He did not say self-sacrifice was a duty, but just "greater love hath no man than this . . ." In fact the word duty occurs only once in the gospels, and then in a somewhat slighting context.

Returning to the Greeks, it appears that they achieved the good life not through a sense of duty but through the more passionate call of beauty of soul. Their attitude to life was less moral than æsthetic: their ideal was a life ordered like an art, and the way to it was the way of art, self-development, not self-repression. Aristotle's category of human virtues contains no reference to dutifulness (it was the Latin poet who made *pietas* the pole-star of his hero). The guiding principle of Aristotle's ethics is to ask not what is man's duty but what is his highest good; and he finds the answer in contemplative happiness.

THE NECESSITY OF HAPPINESS

My purpose is not to disparage duty, but to place it relative to happiness: to suggest that unless doing your duty makes you and others happy it is something other than duty that you are doing. Duty is to be done, but the first of all duties is the great and difficult duty of happiness. A wise woman of our day has urged that people should "build up in themselves the courage to be happy". The great Bishop Butler, who still enjoys a reputation for clear thinking, assumed throughout his arguments the human right to happiness. Yet the notion dies hard that it is wrong to seek happiness for yourself though right to try to make others happy. Trying to make others happy is often just ill-judged interference: better be happy yourself and trust to infection. "The aim", says *The Root and the Flower*, "is not altruism but self-discipline: no man can help his fellow save by the force of his example, by the spectacle of his achieved holiness." The terms are those of religion, but in the philosophy of the East (of which L. H. Myers's remarkable novel is a vehicle) holiness is almost identified with happiness.

Like duty and good works, suffering is held up as a necessity, a blessing, an ideal. The widespread existence of suffering seems to the devotional mind to call for not only acceptance but beatification. Suffering is seen as a sign of grace, and discomfort as a necessary proof of duty done. "This is Christian piety", says Evelyn Underhill, "to renounce and deny everything, in order to serve God—and then to have to suffer for it; to do good and have to suffer for it." As a counsel of despair this will pass: for those whose life is endless suffering, and for whom there is no way out, it is best to bow the head and say, "Evil be thou my good; suffering be thou my joy". Otherwise it is simply neurotic. Apart from the exalted (and therefore perhaps justifiable) mystic attitude just illustrated, people professionally or in other ways concerned to vindicate the existence and ubiquity of suffering contend that suffering is an essential factor in the moral development of human nature. Against this you have the opinion of an acute and perhaps more disinterested observer (Mary Agnes Hamilton) that "good people under great suffering simply go bad". This view can be supported from general experience, but it is equally true that people who have had next to no suffering at all often go bad in an even more unwholesome way. From this it would seem to follow that suffering (like wealth) should be more evenly distributed: no one should have too much, but all should have some. In practice this would mean abolish suffering in every way possible, for there is a "hard core" which is in no danger of being eliminated from life. There will always be enough unavoidable suffering to test that "capacity for suffering" which de Selincourt noted in Dorothy Wordsworth, adding that such capacity for suffering is "the price all must pay for real happiness". The significant phrase is "capacity for". A man may have a large and useful capacity for liquor and yet be well advised not to exceed a modest pint a day. We need too a capacity for happiness, and happiness is an even greater factor in moral development.

Let us start again, with that amazing sentence in *War and Peace*, where Tolstoy speaks of "the highest pitch of happiness, when one becomes completely good and kind, and disbelieves in the very existence of evil and sorrow". By amazing I mean penetrating and illuminating to an almost superhuman degree. At least the observation seems to me to provide an analysis of experience of which few besides Tolstoy would be capable. Our excellent "Erewhon" Butler, subtle and clear-visioned but without the huge genius of the Russian, went only so far as to declare that happy people are "better and more lovable" than those who are unhappy. This is very sound, but Butler's taint of cynicism made him incapable of taking the idea of goodness in Tolstoy's exalted sense, the sense indicated with scrupulous nicety by the chosen expressions—"when one becomes completely good and kind, and disbelieves in the very existence of evil and sorrow". If there is truth in this judgment of Tolstoy's, it would seem to call for some modification of the contempt generally felt for hedonism as an ethical principle. The pursuit of happiness may or may not be a likely way of achieving happiness, but if happiness is in itself so great a good, there can be (as the American Fathers knew) nothing intrinsically wrong in its pursuit. "*Carpe diem* is not", said Chesterton, "the philosophy of happy men: great joy does not gather rosebuds while it may; its eyes are fixed on that immortal rose which Dante saw." I do not like to differ with G.K.C. in spiritual matters, yet an immortal rose should have immortal rosebuds; and if great joy neglects to gather these it is by so much the less joyful.

Young people are taught, or half-taught, many things. How if they should be taught the technique of life, which is the technique of happiness? The hoary maxim, "be good—or work hard, or what-not—and let happiness take care of itself", has resulted in nine people out of ten realising on their death-beds that they have not more than once or twice in their lives come within hailing distance of happiness. And this because of a theory that happiness is either easy and will come of itself, or hard and not worth striving for. It is so well worth while that unless you have found it your life has been a failure, and if you have it you must on no account let it go. Happiness is not easy to achieve, and is still more difficult to keep—its price, like that of liberty, is eternal vigilance. It is for everyone to work out his own "technique", but one rule will be common to every scheme of happiness—to take an intense and tireless interest in every aspect of the never-ending spectacle of life. In spite of the fun that has been poked at Pater's advice to his disciples to "burn always with a hard, gem-like flame", I believe it still provides a clue to the labyrinth of happiness. In practice it means—don't let life ever grow dull upon you, even in its familiar details; do everything you do with lively interest and enjoyment. Two fragments from the poets occur to me in support of the idea. One of the "holier" of the Caroline lyrists said,

> Who sweeps a room as for Thy laws
> Makes that and the action fine.

Irreligious people call that morbid, and many will similarly see an aspect of fatuousness in the suggestion that vital pleasure can be got from the trivial round endlessly repeated. Perhaps more force will be admitted in Walter de la Mare's passionate and inspired cry,

> Look thy last on all things lovely
> Every hour.

But that is a receipt for wringing the last fine agony of joy out of life which can be used only by those who have passed through the bitterness of death itself.

Life has a meaning, if we can but find it; it is meaningless if we cannot. Most people, for lack of it, flounder through a disordered life, not knowing what they want and dissatisfied with most of what they get. Rightly employed, the ideal of happiness might direct and shape such lives as these. The moralists, again, point to other things, less obviously attractive but not therefore more worthy, as giving a meaning to life—generally work, or duty, or self-sacrifice. But the meaning of life can surely not be work! Work, in its common significance, is to happiness as breathing is to life—a necessity, yet breathing is not life, and work is not happiness, and life is more than work. H. W. Nevinson quotes an Aristotelian definition of happiness—the exercise of vital powers along lines of excellence, in a world affording them scope. This seems to me a cause of happiness rather than happiness itself: indeed it provides an admirable definition of *work* as it ideally should be. Yet life must mean more even than this. A man might be engaged on work of this order, but if there were neither love nor God nor peace in his soul he would not be happy. None of these things, work and duty and self-sacrifice, is an end in itself, though they are all very good moral tonics. There is nothing intrinsically good about duty or self-sacrifice: indeed, if their motive, or their result, is a smug satisfaction they are obviously bad, meriting Shaw's satiric comment, "Self-sacrifice enables us to sacrifice other people without blushing". So too if they make other people unhappy. Dorothy Wordsworth complained that Mary's "disposition of self-sacrifice" prevented her from taking care of her health, "though she sees and knows how uneasy it makes us". One of Charles Morgan's characters "couldn't endure that any of life's rooms should be cluttered up with self-sacrifice". Duty is best considered as an aspect of happiness. Duty and happiness are harmonised when a happy man performs duties not as duties but as expressions of happiness. Kant's principle that an action cannot be called good if it is done from natural inclination is to me simply desperate, and I am glad it was our English Ruskin who countered with his blunt assertion that "taste is the only morality".

Life is good. This is a constant, known without argument by those who fully live, and entering as a factor into all true philosophies. Mr. Middleton Murry has found "the fundamental problem of all philosophy worthy of the name" to be the answer to the question, Is life worth living? As foolish a question as to ask a hungry man if roast beef and baked potatoes are worth eating. The fundamental question is—has life a meaning? and what is the meaning of life? Only the happy man can answer those questions with confidence. Happiness alone gives a meaning to life, and the meaning of life is happiness. Love and God are other, and good, answers, but even love and God give but a tragic meaning to life if they do not bring happiness. A life that is happy has unity, pattern, purpose; it satisfies; it is felt to be playing its part in the broad, upward-flowing stream of the greater life; whereas (says Walter de la Mare, striking out a magically brief and right definition)—

> Loving delight forgot,
> Life's very roots must rot.

In *The Excursion* Wordsworth calls happiness "life's genuine inspiration", and Coleridge regarded joy as "the indispensable condition of creative genius". The condition attaches with almost equal necessity to the half-creative work of the priest, the teacher, the doctor, the statesman, and the true craftsman of any kind. It is this creative, imaginative aspect of happiness that explains its independence of duty, work and the rest: if these things are there they are effects not causes—are expressions of the creative impulse of happiness itself. We have seen how Wordsworth's sense of oneness with nature and God gave him the sense of creative power in the soul. So the happy man, feeling himself in harmony with the creative life of the world, feels also to have some share in the creative function, even if he be doing nothing more than stand tip-toe on a little hill. To understand is a kind of creation, and Wordsworth said only a happy man could fully understand his poetry, while Coleridge declared that joy,

> wedding Nature to us, gives in dower
> A new heaven and a new earth
> Undreamt of by the sensual and the proud.

The supreme importance of happiness as a basis of a working philosophy lies in the fact that it is an absolute, and perhaps the only moral absolute that we can know. Can we know beauty, truth, or goodness in this way? Plato thought we could apprehend absolute beauty, but beauty lies in the eye of the beholder. Truth certainly is always relative to knowledge. And if there is no God, asked a writer the other day (and he meant a God whose laws are "revealed" in writing), where shall we find absolute standards of righteousness? But perfect happiness is possible. Not now, of course, except in moments. Yet a moment is a true sample of eternity. And let the peoples of the world once get together and agree upon a few simple principles the operation of which will remove the causes of mass-suffering, then will perfect happiness be attainable by those individuals who have the gift of happiness: happiness known to be perfect, unconditional, absolute. Even before such happiness becomes possible it can be imagined. We cannot even imagine perfect truth or perfect beauty. Perfect goodness is further still from our comprehension, because we do not know what goodness is except under the simplest conditions. What action would represent perfect goodness in the face of industrialism or Hitlerism?

But he who has once been happy, says Scawen Blunt—

> He who has once been happy is for aye
> Out of destruction's reach. His fortune then
> Holds nothing secret, and Eternity,
> Which is a mystery to other men,

THE NECESSITY OF HAPPINESS

    Has like a woman given him its joy.
      Time is his conquest. Life, if it should fret,
    Has paid him tribute. He can bear to die,
      He who has once been happy!

And he who has achieved lasting happiness has within himself an absolute standard by which to measure all the other "goods"; he is, as Plato says, peculiarly independent of external resources. Indeed, happiness might seem to be Plato's absolute good, that absolute good which he believed could be known only by the mind withdrawn in contemplation from the body. I believe absolute good can be known through the passion of happiness, proceeding from the spirit which loves and adores, the mind which finds God through a wise passiveness, the heart which is sensitive to the subtle emanations of life, the bodily frame which pulses with the crude glad appetites of earth. Through happiness the plain man can come, as Walt Whitman did, to mystic experience.

It is worth while pausing to note that Whitman, like Wordsworth (and much more stridently), made the unusual claim to happiness. He said that *Leaves of Grass* was an attempt to put a happy man into literature, and in one of the poems he exclaims, "Who has been happiest? O I think it is I—I think no one was ever happier than I!" His happiness is a much simpler state than Wordsworth's. The "pleasure that there is in life itself" is more than central with Whitman—it is nearly everything. Health plus freedom makes up the greater part of Whitman's happiness, with intense mental activity coming in as a late afterthought. For this reason Whitman's "mysticism" is incomplete: arising from his sheer zest for life it never, or seldom, gets through to God. Whitman is his own God—"there is nothing more wonderful than I myself". But in the limited sense of intuitive contact with the universal life of the world his mysticism is true. It specially embraces universalised human life. Wordsworth was keenly aware of this too, but used it as a means to his grasp of the divine life.

The practical value of happiness as an absolute lies in the

conception of joy as an index of moral health. In happiness we have an unchanging and infallible criterion of right action, right relation, right life. If your work, your relations with God and man, your way of life do not bring you and others happiness, they are futile and wrong, however strenuous and well-intentioned and apparently productive they may be. If happiness all round does arise from these things they are right, even if not obviously useful. When Lord Samuel says that actions must be judged good or bad according to their consequences, Mr. L. P. Jacks asks by what criterion those consequences are to be judged. One might answer (a) have they moved, or tended to move, life upward and onward? (b) have they meant happiness in the lives of those actively and passively concerned? Often an answer to (a) can be inferred only from the answer to (b). And if it be asked how true happiness is to be known, the reply to that question has long ago been given: unless it comprehends love, peace, and a sense of participation in the vast spiritual life of the world it is not happiness but a profitless simulacrum.

By reason of its position as an absolute, and of its nature as the divinest condition of the soul, happiness is an index, a criterion, and a criticism of the good life, which is life in harmony with the ascending spirit of the universe, life in living contact with God. In *The Brothers Karamazov*, Zossima the Elder says, "Men are made for happiness, and anyone who is completely happy has a right to say to himself, 'I am doing God's will on earth'".

For happiness, like any other principle of life, must ultimately justify itself by its accordance with the will of God. And happiness is able to do this by reason of its being a means of contact with God, which implies at least some measure of knowledge of the will of God. Contrary to the opinion of most leaders of religious thought, contact with God is to be achieved in more than one way, and it is the achievement and maintenance of contact with God, by whatever means, that constitutes the religious life. "Revelation" is indeed necessary, but "all truth", said Coleridge, "is a species of revelation", and the field of revelation is as wide as life itself. It comprises not only the

THE NECESSITY OF HAPPINESS

writings of great Churchmen, the Hebrew Scriptures, and the teaching of Jesus, but in addition all great poetry and prose, art and science, the world of nature, mystical experience which comes out of contemplation, and happiness born of love. Someone has said that virtue is an essential preliminary to the mystical experience: this may well be, but happiness is another preliminary. It is not that out of religion come virtue and happiness, but that out of virtue and happiness comes religion. Happiness is a form of mystical experience, a way of contact with that absolute reality, that supreme and eternal truth, which is God. "The knowledge of God is better than happiness", says Bernard Shaw, but (as is so often the case with Shaw when he gets above a certain level of thought) he is expressing only half the truth: the knowledge of God *is* happiness, and happiness is the knowledge of God.

To the professional mystics and the theologians all that I am saying here will be foolishness. Nevertheless, without "daily exercises" of the sort recommended by Krishnamurti, or the arduous training which has for its end "the mystical union of the soul with the integrating principle", I believe that some such union can come about in the lives of most people at moments when the soul is in a condition of exaltation induced by love or contemplation; that many of us can know

> that serene and blessed mood
> In which the affections gently lead us on,
> Until, the breath of this corporeal frame
> And even the motion of our human blood
> Almost suspended, we are laid asleep
> In body, and become a living soul:
> While . . . we see into the life of things;

and that a lower but adequate degree of exaltation can be almost continuously present, and the mystical union in a milder form maintained almost unbroken, when life is interpenetrated with happiness. "To be in love", says Aldous Huxley, "is to have achieved a state of being in which it becomes possible to have direct intuition of the essentially lovely nature of all reality"; and this implies a mystical union. We have already noted that "being in love" is at once too narrow and too loose a term to cover the requisite condition. Yet happiness is a synonym for being in love—with a woman, with life, with "the essentially lovely nature of all reality". For normal people, vital touch with God is most readily maintained through happiness. In fact happiness *is* the vital touch; happiness is a sense of God. Even one may feel that happiness is God: that happiness is that attribute of the divine reality into which human nature can most completely enter.

The happy man, having achieved through happiness contact with reality and consciousness of participation in the life of an immanent God, may adopt what creed his mind and tastes prefer; it is obvious that the creed must be a spiritual one; full happiness does not run with materialism. But it seems also to me that at this day the creed of the happy man must include an explanation of the fact of evil other than the ordinary theological explanations, which are nothing more than confessions that evil cannot be explained within the scheme of Christian theology. To be happy in face of the fact of evil one must see it as a necessary concomitant of the as yet incomplete evolution of God. The end and motive of evolution is the perfection of God. There is, says Whitehead, a process inherent in God's nature whereby his infinity is acquiring realisation. Until that infinitely distant end and realisation have been reached the scheme of things, which is life, must be full of loose ends, designs unfinished and gone wrong, errors in conception, effects unwilled and undesired, all to be righted with experience and the growth of wisdom and power in God. Happiness requires that God should be seen as perfect love but limited in power and wisdom—at least in power. Man's strivings towards beauty and truth are part of the evolution of God: neither can be without the other: God needs man's help as man needs God's. Hence the joy of the sense, afforded by happiness, of participation in the life of God. Wordsworth, of course, belongs to an earlier age. Like Plato, he saw the divine idea, the abstract and ultimate perfection, with such clearness that he gave little heed to the flaws of execution which to us seem at least to require explanation. Plato put them aside as transitory and accidental; Wordsworth called them "passing shows of Being". Such indeed they are, but not the less pressing for us who must also pass. To see evil steadily, and to see it aright, is as necessary to happiness as health, or as happiness itself is to a full and complete life.

Index of Quotations

(To save space, the first word only of each quotation is given, and initials are used for works frequently quoted: P=*Prelude*—1805 version unless otherwise indicated; E=*Excursion*; R=*Recluse Bk. I*; T.A.=*Tintern Abbey Lines*; W.D.=*White Doe of Rylstone*; V.J.=*Vaudracour and Julia*; L=Letters—from W. W. except where D.W. indicates from Dorothy.)

Page
1 by ... E. I, 516–19.
2 He ... L. D.W. to Lady Beaumont, Mar. 17, 1805.
5 There ... P. XI, 258–60.
6 When ... P. IV, 137–41.
   a simple ... R. 808.
   little ... T.A. 34–5.
   the wisest ... *By the Side of Rydal Mere*, 37.
7 attuned ... P. XI, 209–11.
   Having ... *Composed by the Sea-shore*, 32–3.
   A pleasurable ... *Michael*, 76–7.
11 genial ... L. to W. R. Hamilton, June 6, 1832.
   having ... P. X, 869–71.
12 Was ... P. I, 271–82.
13 Oh, many ... P. I, 291–302.
   a golden ... P. V, 503.
   repeating ... P. V, 588.
   easily ... P. V, 433–5.
14 We ... P. II, 48–9.
   I ... P. I, 502–4.
   We were ... P. (1850) I, 479–82.

Page
   in happiness ... P. V, 403–4.
15 I was ... P. III, 28–9.
   my ... P. III, 235–6.
   invitations ... P. III, 41.
   I was ... P. III, 89–90.
   I had ... P. III, 142–3.
   a childlike ... P. III, 148.
   The Poet's ... P. VI, 55–7.
16 And yet ... P. VI, 63–4.
   an act ... P. VI, 40.
   a treasured ... P. VI, 196–8.
   In summer ... P. VI, 208–13.
17 benevolence ... P. VI, 368–9.
   thirteen ... L. to D.W. Oct. 6, 1790.
   I needed ... P. VI, 700–5.
18 Free ... P. XI, 18.
   motley ... P. VII, 150–3.
   I quitted ... L. to Mathews, June 17, 1791.
   I did ... P. VIII, 597–605.
19 Tranquil ... P. IX, 87–8.
20 O pleasant ... P. X, 690–4.

124

INDEX

21 the effect ... V.J. 54–6.
Arabian ... V.J. 39–53.
22 Each ... P. IX, 573–4.
a stolen ... V.J. 85–101.
23 Action ... *Borderers*, 1539–42.
24 All ... P. X, 899–901.
25 The immortal ... *Misc. Sonnets* VI.
the most ... L. D.W. to Jane Pollard, April, 1794.
26 Oh, there, etc. P. I, 1–21.
27 to make ... L. D.W. to Jane Marshall, Mar. 19, 1797.
the beloved ... P. (1850). XI, 335–42.
28 She ... P. X, 919–21.
29 he was ... (and next) D.W. to Jane Pollard, July 10, 1793.
30 inwardly ... P. XI, 3–7.
the complete ... P. I, 121–2.
from ... P. (1850) I, 112–13. William ... L. D.W. to Jane Marshall, Mar. 19, 1797.
31 Predestined ... P. VI, 267–9.
32 William's ... L. D.W. to Mary H., Mar. 5, 1797.
regulate ... day P. X, 908–930.
33 in ... P. XI, 31–34.
still ... P. XI, 192.
wise ... P. XI, 205–14.
in ... P. XI, 256–7.
35 you will ... L. to D.W. Nov. 7, 1799.
36 A termination ... R. 147–50.
And now ... R. 59.
On Nature's ... R. 82.
37 Mine eyes ... R. 94.
The boon ... R. 103.
38 He writes ... L. D.W. to Mrs. Marshall, Sep. 10, 1800.
41 others ... R. 657–61.
42 in ... P. (1850) X, 415.
44 We were ... D.W's *Journal of an Excursion on the Banks of Ullswater*.
46 deprived ... L. to J.K. Miller, Dec. 17, 1831.
47 I ... L. to Ida Fenwick, May 13, 1846.
55 realities ... R. 65–8.
Dust ... P. (1850) 340–50.
57 The Poet ... P. I, 145–56.
60 We ... E. IV, 763.
61 I ... P. VI, 77–9.
A love ... P. XIII, 162–5.
By love ... P. XIII, 149–52.
62 So ... P. VIII, 171–2.
63 of little ... P. XIII, 209–10.
the thoughts ... L. to Beaumont, Mar. 1807.
Life ... E. V, 1002.
For ... P. VIII, 69–70.
A Freeman ... P. VIII, 386 and 394.
64 Immense ... P. VIII, 46–58.
in ... P. X, 578–9.
and spread ... P. X, 838–9.
65 vast ... P. VIII, 836–40.
suffering ... *Borderers*, 1543–4.
66 in ... E. I, 366–71.
67 blessed ... P. XIII, 437–9.
a thousand ... P. XIII, 447–8.
68 Through ... P. XI, 31–4.
a more ... P. IV, 164–5.
the silent ... E. I, 189.
those ... P. XII, 51–2.
69 For ... E. III, 381–2.
a happy ... P. XII, 13.
The mind ... P. I, 351–5.

INDEX

70 Incumbencies . . . P. III, 115–18.
  yet . . . P. V, 473–7.
71 Pre-eminent . . . *There was a Boy*, 28–34.
  The surface . . . P. I, 499–501.
72 The pulse . . . P. VIII, 626.
  the deep . . . P. XIII, 261.
  exalted . . . P. XIII, 71–2.
74 Rapt . . . E. I, 215–16.
75 one . . . P. (1850) VIII, 630.
  VIII, 484.
  Was . . . P. (1850) XIII, 150.
76 Worked . . . P. I, 419.
  A second . . . P. VII, 601.
  even . . . P. I, 613.
  a gentle . . . P. V, 407.
  the ghostly . . . P. II, 328.
  Appeared . . . P. XIII, 68.
77 Most . . . P. II, 432.
  his . . . E. I, 206.
78 By . . . P. XIII, 103.
  for I . . . P. (1850) II, 302.
79 with bliss . . . P. II, 419.
  for there . . . P. VIII, 834.
  out of . . . P. XIII, 183.
  exalted . . . P. XIII, 71.
80 the one . . . de Selincourt's Introduction, §10.
81 for . . . R. 805–8.
  worlds . . . R. 782–96.
  How . . . R. 816.
  prophetic . . . R. 836–40.
82 sometimes . . . E. I, 409.
84 the Eternal . . . de Selincourt's notes, 508.
  Great . . . P. X, 386.
  Our . . . P. VI, 538.
  Wisdom . . . P. I, 428.
85 curious . . . E. IV, 1132–87.
86 at this . . . P. I, 517.
88 Oh what . . . E. IV, 532.
89 many . . . P. II, 191.
90 Thus did . . . P. IV, 385–99.

when . . . P. (1850) VI, 600.
Those . . . P. I, 578.
91 well-pleased . . . T.A. 107.
92 A countenance . . . *Phantom of Delight*.
93 grew . . . P. I, 305.
  The soul . . . P. VII, 736.
  Beauty . . . R. 795–800.
94 sweep . . . E. IX, 137.
  more . . . P. II, 299.
  When . . . P. II, 305.
95 An auxiliar . . . P. II, 387.
96 Bleak . . . R. 152.
  with . . . R. 172.
  I felt . . . P. XI, 238.
97 nature . . . P. I, 572.
  hallowed . . . P. I, 578.
  vows . . . P. IV, 341–4.
  in its . . . P. IV, 366.
98 huge . . . P. I, 425.
99 Yet I . . . P. I, 604.
  Look . . . R. 441.
  The elements . . . P. VIII, 148.
  the fragrance . . . P. VIII, 151–8.
  the bliss . . . P. XII, 129.
  Converse . . . P. XII, 141.
100 a little . . . P. VII, 23–48.
  the patient . . . R. 709.
101 The inferior . . . P. VIII, 490.
  the purest . . . W.D. 1852–3.
102 To the . . . W.D. 1596–7.
  With a . . . W.D. 1757–8.
  When she . . . W.D. 1821–4.
103 If this . . . T.A. 49–57.
  If this . . . P. II, 435.
  The gift . . . P. II, 461.
  remembers . . . L. D.W. to Mrs. Clarkson, Jan. 10, 1817.
106 In common . . . *Poet's Grave*.

INDEX

106 led ... P. (1850) XI, 352.
Meanwhile ... E. IV, 627.
107 Now ... P. II, 298–306.
starting ... P. VIII, 456.
intellectual ... P. XI, 43.
feeling ... P. XIII, 205.
108 Our ... *Immortality Ode*.
Never ... *Hartleap Well*.
the very ... P. XI, 144.
those ... *Immortality Ode*.
Come ... *Tables Turned*.
Myself ... *Three Years She Grew*.
109 a spirit ... *Phantom of Delight*.
Then ... *Nutting*.
117 life's ... E. III, 423.
121 that serene ... T.A.

Index of Poems
(reference beyond quotation)

Borderers, The, 23.
Brougham Castle, 67–8.
Castle of Indolence, The, 40.
Cuckoo, To the, 1, 100.
Duty, Ode to, 65, 66–7.
Early Spring, Lines Written in, 8.
Evening Walk, An, 16.
Excursion, The, 2, 51–3, 66, 72–5, 81–3, 85, 87–8, 117.
Expostulation and Reply, 69.
Happy Warrior, The, 3.
Hartleap Well, 58.
Home at Grasmere (see *The Recluse*).
Immortality Ode, 58–9, 106.
Lyrical Ballads, 31, 35, 48, 54, 74.
Michael, 7.
O Nightingale, 4.
Peel Castle, 65.
Phantom of Delight, She was a, 92.
Prelude, The, passim.
Recluse, The, Bk. I. (*Home at Grasmere*), 31, 36–7, 41, 49 50, 80–1, 85, 93, 96.
Slumber Did, A, 109.
Tables Turned, The, 104.
There is a ... Rill, 35.
There was a Boy, 71.
Thorn, The, 55.
Three Years She Grew, 91.
Tintern Abbey Lines, 33–4, 72, 85, 89, 106, 110.
Vaudracour and Julia, 20–22.
White Doe of Rylstone, The, 54, 65–6, 101–2.

General Index

Animals, 100–1.
Annette, (see Vallon).
Aristotle, 112, 116.
"Blind Love", 3, 7, 28, 61.
Browning, R., 88.
Coleridge, S.T., 3, 18, 27, 30–2

INDEX

34–5, 38, 39, 44–5, 50, 52–4, 56, 63, 73, 95, 101, 105, 107, 117, 118, 120.
Coleridge, Sara, 47, 74.
"Composition Sickness", 34, 38,
de la Mare, W., 57, 60, 115, 117.
de Quincey, 87, 92.
de Selincourt, E., viii, 41, 50, 52, 58, 80, 114.
Dostoievsky, 120.
Dunn, S. G., 85.
Evil, 55, 122–3.
Fear, 98.
France, 16–17, 19–23.
Freedom, 12–15.
Garrod, 5, 23.
Grasmere, 35 et seq., 64, 100.
Hardy, T., 78–9.
Harper, G. M., 19, 30, 44, 62, 101.
Havens, R. D. (*The Mind of a Poet*), 98, 110.
Herford, C. H., 59, 77.
Hutchinson, Mary (see Mary Wordsworth).
Immanence, 71–81, 84.
Lin Yutang, 2, 44.
Lamb, C., 28, 35, 99, 101.
Langbridge, Rosamond, 86.
"Later poems", 50–1.
Love Poetry, 29, 36–7, 62, 91–2.
"Lucy", 62, 91.
Marriage, 40–2.
Morgan, C., 69, 70, 116.

Mysticism, 75–8, 84, 90, 92, 113, 119, 121.
Nature, 93–9 and *passim*.
"Nature's holy plan", 8–10.
Pantheism, 10, 85.
Plato, 94, 118, 119, 122–3.
Raleigh, W., 55, 102.
Robinson, Crabb, 1, 11, 46, 73.
Ruskin, 96, 117.
Shakespeare, 21, 57, 110.
Shaw, G. B., 104–5, 121.
Smith, J. C., 29, 98.
Socrates, 92, 103.
Solitude, 97.
Suffering, 65–6.
Tagore, R., 10, 86.
Temperament, 12–13.
Tolstoy, 43, 105, 114.
Tragedy, 54–7.
Transcendence, 81–3.
Upanishads, 10, 72.
Vallon, Annette, 20–24, 41–2, 62.
Walking, 17, 24, 25, 26, 87–8.
Wanderer, The, 72, 73, 74, 75, 77, 82, 87, 94.
Whitehead, A. N., 69, 73, 92, 107.
Whitman, W., 119.
Wordsworth, Dorothy, 2, 7, Chap. II *passim*, 62, 63, 66, 96, 103, 114, 116.
  Journals of, 5, 28, 37–43.
Wordsworth, Mary, 38, 40–2, 44, 62, 116.